$22

THE COMPLETE
SIAMESE CAT

THE COMPLETE
SIAMESE CAT

Milo G. Denlinger

Illustrated

1975—Ninth Printing

HOWELL BOOK HOUSE INC.

730 Fifth Avenue

New York, N.Y. 10019

Contents

CAT HEAD
Bronze; late Egyptian, 7th-4th century B. C.
Lent by The Brooklyn Museum

Foreword

ALL owners of Siamese Cats will welcome this delightful and authoritative guide to the breed of their choice.

I am particularly impressed with Mr. Denlinger's research into the origin and history of the Siamese Cat because this information is difficult to obtain. He has also captured the character of this regal breed in a word description the most ardent devotee will find wholly satisfying.

The illustrations represent a priceless gallery of Siamese lore appealing both to the expert breeder and fond pet owner. The fancier will recognize many of the outstanding producers pictured on the following pages; the pet owner will appreciate the many typical posings shown, especially the utterly charming "dance" sequence depicted between pages 72 and 73.

The ever-growing popularity of the Siamese Cat calls for just such a definitive work as this. As a breeder, exhibitor, and admirer of this fascinating animal, I am happy to commend THE COMPLETE SIAMESE CAT to all.

Mrs. John W. Hoag
President, 1959-1961
Empire Cat Club

"WANT OUT"
Modern Print by Agnes Tait

Reproduced courtesy The Cooper Union Museum for the Arts of
Decoration, New York City, and CATS Magazine, Pittsburgh, Pa.

The Siamese Cat

HE Siamese cat is a true cat, a *Felis lybyca domestica,* responsive to the same treatment and management as the other varieties of the domestic cat, neither more hardy nor more delicate than other cats as a lot (despite allegations of the comparative frailty of the Siamese), and with all the common feline natures and attributes. It must be granted that in certain particulars the Siamese differs from other cat breeds sufficiently to set it off as a breed apart from others, but even in such particulars the Siamese violates none of the principles of feline structure and nature. Wherein the Siamese tribe may vary as a lot from the other domestic cats, it will be found that individuals in the other breeds may conform in some particulars and to some degree closer to the Siamese than to the mill-run of the members of their own respective breeds.

Siamese cats are interfertile with other domestic cats, and the hybrids are fertile to either back-cross or to a mating with some other variety or breed. This is shown by the production of cats with the coat pattern of the Siamese together with the more rounded skull, shorter body, and shorter legs that pertain to occidental domestic cats. Through selection for color and coat, it has even been possible to isolate long-haired cats with the markings of the Siamese and a pseudo race of Siamese with the points red rather than seal-brown. Genetically speaking, the Siamese color pattern is recessive to the tabby and whole-colored cats, and the first cross of the Siamese with cats of other colors does not result in kittens with the Siamese pattern; this requires back-crosses to the Siamese or to some other cat that harbors the gene or genes for the Siamese pattern. This will be discussed at greater length elsewhere in this book.

Wherein do Siamese cats so differ from other varieties of domestic cats that the uninformed are given to consider them a separate and distinct species, some prone to consider them a separate family and not cats at all? First, Siamese are totally white at the time of their birth, changing their color gradually and reaching their fully pigmented pattern only at maturity, with the body coat continuing to darken up until two and even three or four years of age. The fact is that many other varieties of cats deepen or change in color as they mature, although none alters so markedly as the Siamese. This is true of dogs also, the Dalmatian dog being white until maturity and the Yorkshire Terrier being born almost totally black and fading to steel-gray on his saddle later in his life. The Himalayan rabbit, whose color pattern so closely resembles that of the Siamese cat, is also totally white when littered. These alterations in color and pattern between birth and maturity do not hinder the acceptance of the Dalmatian and the Yorkshire Terrier as authentic breeds of dogs or of the Himalayan as a true breed of rabbit. There exists no reason why the absence of pigmentation at the time of its birth should set the Siamese apart as a species from other domestic breeds of cats.

Moreover, much is made of the devotion of the Siamese cat to its human owner and its love of human companionship. Many persons consider that in such respect he is

10

more like a dog than like a cat. It is true that the Siamese enjoys human company, human sympathy, and human attentions more, as a lot, than do most other breeds of cats. However, there are individual cats of other breeds that evince an equal love for and dependence upon humans to those of the Siamese. And the Siamese's devotion is never dog-like. Like other cats, the Siamese is never servile; he never fawns. He may cater to or flatter his human master, but it is always for a purpose, to beg for food or to be let out or in doors, or for some other thing he may want. But even then he does not truckle. When he has achieved his end, he resumes his independence of spirit and his liberty of action. He is never at the human beck or call and can be very recalcitrant to human wishes. The dog, if he can be made to understand what is demanded of him, will do it. The cat may understand well enough but he will perform only if the impulse moves him. The Siamese can rather easily be taught to do tricks, but just try to make him exhibit them if he is not in the mood to do so!

There is no denial of the attachment of the Siamese cat to his human associates, but the man is not the master. The Siamese is master. He wants what he wants when he wants it, and usually manages by his pleading (otherwise by stealth or by outright and arrant theft) to obtain it.

And how he can plead! He is so vocal with his incessant yowling and mewing that he drives a person forced to listen to him almost to distraction. He talks all the time he is awake. There is little doubt that he tries to, and often succeeds in conveying a meaning with his sometimes raucous and always persistent voice. There are frequent alterations in the tone, pitch, timbre, and volume of that voice, as if he were seeking to converse on various topics, grave or gay, tragic or comical. One feels that he is endeavoring to make clear whatever is on his mind; and, if he is begging for something, he employs gestures as well as "words" to make certain what he wants one to do. There can be no doubt that the Siamese is more loquacious than other breeds of cats, but his meows are only more numerous and more expressive than those of other cats;

not different. Indeed, this constant chatter is one of the faults of the breed, and if one is to possess a Siamese one simply has to put up with his incessant conversation.

Another count upon which the Siamese breed is presumably different from other cats is that the Siamese male or tomcat, despite his violence and proclivities to fight with other toms of whatever breed, is prone to be tolerant toward and gentle with young kittens. This is not unique with the breed, for an occasional tom of some other breed may be kind to his own kittens or those of some other cat; and it is not a universal trait among Siamese toms. However, the natures of most tomcats move them to menace or destroy whatever kittens they may find, but most Siamese toms are disposed to tolerate, even to fondle and play with, their young of whatever age.

All mammalian species produce more male than female progeny, although the males are more backward in their development and maturity than the females and more of them die in infancy. This high mortality among the males in most species results in an approximate equality of the numbers of the respective sexes at maturity. Although this law or tendency holds good among all the mammalia, of which there has been statistical observation, as we have said, including the domestic cats, the greater ratio of male to female births among Siamese cats is particularly marked. Most litters of Siamese cats include so many more males than females that it has been informally estimated that there are littered approximately twice as many male kittens as females, and breeds of Siamese generally recognize that the males are more delicate and require more care in their rearing. No valid statistic about this ratio is available and none can be compiled, but the larger preponderance of male births in Siamese than in other cat varieties is impossible to doubt.

If we were able to predict that every litter of Siamese kittens would contain twice as many males as females, the fact might be sufficient for the taxonomists to classify the Siamese as a species separate from the other cats; but this does not occur. There have been many litters of Siamese

12

that contained more females than males, and even a few litters that were of females only, which does not invalidate the fact that in the aggregate many more males are born.

No satisfactory explanation or reason has been put forth for the great disparity in the numbers of the sexes in the particular variety of cats, and there is no known way to predetermine or to regulate the numbers. The phenomenon, however, is not a justification to declare the Siamese to be a separate species rather than a distinct variety of cat.

As for the difference of the Siamese in type and structure from other cats, it is not so great as the difference of the Dachshund from the Greyhound, both dogs; or as that of the Thoroughbred from the Shire, both horses; or as that of the Jersey from the Hereford, both cattle. The ideal type of the Siamese varies from that of the occidental cat, it is to be admitted, but the variation violates none of the determiners of type for the domestic cat.

We must then classify the Siamese as a breed or variety of the domestic cat, *Felis lybyca domestica,* and not as a separate species as some of its admirers are disposed to do. We shall expand our discussion of Siamese idiosyncrasies in their proper chapters as we go along. Here they are merely mentioned for the purpose of fixing the Siamese for what he is, a household cat.

"Simpkin Came Out of the Tailor's Door"
Water-color drawing, 1902, by Beatrix Potter (1866-1943)
For illustration for *The Tailor of Gloucester*
Lent by the Trustees of the Tate Gallery

The Origin and Status of the Siamese Cat

HERE the first of the cats known in the Occident as Siamese might have come from it is impossible to know. The history of the country, which we again call Siam (although known as Thailand, the land of free men, from 1939 to 1945) yields no clue to the cat. There are several poetic legends about the little beast, but they are so mystical, so patently untrue, that we are forced to assume that they have been from the beginning untrue and not intended to be believed. They are as incredible as the Greek Aphrodite's rising from the sea or Minerva's birth full panoplied from the brow of Zeus.

We are able only to speculate about the origin of the cat, and many have been the persons, unable to find any definite origin, who have indulged in such speculation. It is impossible to be sure that the Siamese cat is even autochthonous to Siam. It is equally reasonable to suppose

15

that it had its orgin elsewhere in southeast Asia, in what are now known as the Malay States, Indo-China, Burma, or the Himalayan region. In any event, it was popular in Siam and appears to have had its concentration in that country.

Credence is lent to a southeast Asiatic origin by the fact that the cats native to the region possess gnarled, crooked, short, or otherwise deformed tails, which are also characteristic of the Siamese in the East and valued there accordingly. The Siamese that have been imported from Siam to England, from the first to come in -1884 up until recently, have had crooks in their tails. The British standard by which Siamese are judged gives the kink in the tail scant approval and most British and American judges consider it to be a definite fault. As a result of the British selection for straight tails, the kink in the tail has been pretty well eliminated in Siamese cats of occidental breeding. However, kinked tails persist in the Orient and are valued as far north as the British colony at Hong Kong.

The similarity of the markings of the Siamese cat to those of the Himalayan rabbit leads one to suspect a similar origin of the two varieties. Such markings do not occur in any other species of which we are aware, and it is just possible that the same people developed the two breeds.

There are numerous varieties of cats, named and un-named, in south and southeastern Asia, notably the Indian cat and the Burma cat, with the general type of the Siamese, long-headed, high on the legs, "svelt" (to quote the Siamese standard), lissome, with long, tapering, gnarled tails. These differ from the Siamese essentially only in their colors and markings. The Siamese with its peculiar color and markings may have been derived from one of these other varieties, and it is probable that it did, as a single mutant. If such is the case, we are fortunate that some fancier recognized the mutant's difference and beauty, and took the breeding in hand to preserve the pattern.

Such experimental breeding to obtain a race of cats with the "points" we now characterize as Siamese must have re-quired several generations, two at the very least, since the Siamese pattern is known to be genetically recessive to

16

SILKEN PEDRO OF BRIDLE TRAIL

Bred in England by Mrs. Denys Highton, owned by Mrs. John W. Hoag, Bridle Trail, Darien, Conn., has sired ten Champions and is the grandsire of many more Champions including six Grand Champions.

This picture illustrates crossed eyes, a fault formerly found in Siamese Cats. This has now been bred out.

SEAL POINT AND BLUE POINT SIAMESE KITTENS
Breeder-Owner: Mr. and Mrs. L. R. Van Riper, Rockville, Maryland.

This photograph illustrates the crooked tails which until recently were
characteristic of the Siamese Cat but has now been bred
out and is considered a fault.

self-patterns and tabbies and for it to manifest itself the genes for it must be carried by both parents. This recessivity was, of course, unknown to the Asiatics at the time of the development of the Siamese cat, and was only discovered in the Occident in the latter half of the nineteenth century. Only by breeding the progeny of the mutant back to it, or by breeding together two of its progeny, could the pattern have been preserved; and this, we may surmise, is what occurred, whether the mating was fortuitous or duly planned. When the breeder had obtained two specimens of opposite sexes, both with the Siamese pattern, the perpetuation of the variety was easy, since the progeny of two similar genetic recessives are always recessive and breed true for the particular attribute. Thus, two mates with the Siamese pattern, whatever their ancestry may be, will invariably produce progeny manifesting that pattern.

We may assume that cats with the Siamese "points" first appeared in Siam or somewhere in southeast Asia, as a mutation, as we have said, from cats of more common or usual color patterns. After such first appearance, it required no long and involved selection to produce a true-breeding variety, which subsequently came to be known as the Siamese.

How the cat itself, distinct from the Siamese, came to southeast Asia is easier to surmise. It is generally known that the cat was a sacred animal to the Egyptians—as early as three thousand years before the Christian era. It is supererogatory here to detail the rites in which the cat was worshiped in Egypt and the custom of mummifying and burying the cats which died. It is believed, but not definitely known, that the Egyptian cats were striped and marked in the manner of our present day tabbies, and that they were the progenitors of the Caffre cat that is so widespread in Africa. It is believed that all the varieties of the domestic cat were also derived from the cats of Egypt.

It is easy to believe that at least some of the Egyptian traders in their commerce with southeastern Asia, which is known to have occurred from very early times, took with

17

them in their ships some of the cats which they and their people worshiped. And it is recognized that the comings and the goings of cats are not easy to control. It appears probable that some of the cats taken along on these voyages escaped from their owners and devotees, or even were stolen from them (since they would not have been sold or easily parted from), and attached themselves to new owners on the Asiatic mainland. We are unable even so much as to guess when the first domestic cat reached Asia, but it is safe to say that it was at least considerably before the eighth, ninth, or tenth centuries when cats (other than the indigenous wildcats) were first known of in the British Isles. A single pair of cats, or even one pregnant female and her brood, would have been sufficient to populate the community through the generations. This is not to allege that the cats that were taken from Egypt by such traders were the Siamese cat as we know it, but they could well account for the presence of domestic cats in Siam and in other parts of Asia. There are records of cats in China so early as 400 B.C., which may have had a similar provenance.

These cats through the centuries and the many generations have evolved and altered in their type and conformation, either through their evolutionary adaptation to their environment or through artificial selection; and in at least one case, notably the Siamese, a new color pattern has arisen.

It is particularly to be noted that the Siamese cat as it is known in the Occident is not the only cat that is to be found in Siam, or even the most numerous. In the Siamese streets and alleys, and even in the houses and compounds, are to be seen gray, and tabby, and black, and spotted cats, just as in the Occident. Possibly only a small part of one percent of the cats in Siam are of the color variety or pattern which we call Siamese, or of any approximation to the Siamese. One is fortunate to find a single specimen of a Siamese cat in a week's journey in Siam. In this respect the Siamese cat in Siam is analogous to the Chihuahua dog in the State of Chihuahua in Mexico

18

where among the numerous mongrels one may search in vain for a Chihuahua.

It has been estimated that Siamese cats are far more numerous in England than in Siam, although it is difficult to determine how such an estimate can be arrived at, since no census of cats in either country has been made and since it is impossible to determine any borderline between Siamese and other varieties of cats that may have some Siamese blood and to classify them distinctly as one thing or the other. The only datum we have is the registration of cats in Great Britain which shows a population of approximately eight thousand purebred Siamese in that country. It may well be doubted that there are an equal number of Siamese cats in Siam, but nobody can say so with any degree of authority and the comparison is to say the least invidious.

The cats in Siam, like the other domestic animals, are neglected and uncared for, neither sheltered nor regularly fed. The people of Siam (or of Thailand, as the country was more recently known) are as a lot members of the Buddhist faith. Buddhists are not permitted to kill animals or deliberately to abuse them, but they may neglect them or ignore their welfare with impunity to their immortal souls. Food is too scarce and the means of living is too difficult to come by in Siam for the natives to waste their substance or their time in their attention to their animals and particularly to animals that serve no other purpose than that of mere pets. This is the reason for the tourist's seeing so many half-starved, dirty, mange-ridden, and sore-eyed cats in that country. We may be prone to blame the people for the conditions of their animals, but in the light of their basic religion, their mores, and their economic status, the starvation, disease, and neglect of their cats is not to be wondered at.

Some persons speak and write of "royal" Siamese cats, as if the possession or breeding of such cats were confined to the royalty of Siam. There is no evidence to show that commoners and other persons are precluded from the rights to keep and breed such animals. Nor can there be

19

doubts that the kings and their relatives have cats and that the royal cats are as a lot better fed and cared for than those of plebeian ownership. The kings have ample food to spare for their cats.

However, we may look for no such royal monopoly of Siamese cats as pertained to Pekingese dogs at the imperial courts of China. Indeed, even if the Siamese kings had been disposed to maintain their cats as a royal prerogative (and there is evidence of no such disposition), it would have been difficult if not impossible of accomplishment. Whereas the Pekingese dogs were a deliberately crippled breed, bred so to prevent their disposition to stray, cats would require to be kept constantly in cages to keep them from roaming and from breeding wherever they could find a mate.

The "royal" as a part of the name for the variety is pure nonsense. It was probably adopted in that end of the nineteenth century in an effort to give some added glamor to the breed at a time when royalty had lost none of its status and prestige that no longer attaches to it.

Many, and indeed most, of the earlier importations of Siamese cats into England in the eighties of the nineteenth century were represented by their owners as being gifts from the King of Siam. Without any categorical claims that all such boasts were insubstantial, we may doubt that many of such importers rated a royal gift or that the Kings of Siam were given to such largess to persons of so little importance as the earlier owners of Siamese cats in England. It may be true that a few of the early Siamese in England came from the royal compound of the King of Siam, but the numbers claiming such a provenience were such as to detract from any distinction that might at the time have attached to such an origin. It appears much more likely that most of the Siamese came from humbler sources.

In any event, English fanciers have changed and bettered the Siamese since the early importations. It is no longer quite the same breed. The framers of the English standard for Siamese cats, by which the breed is presumably judged

20

in occidental shows, have made such concessions to the kink in the tails so characteristic of Asiatic cats as to specify that tails may be straight or crooked. However, the judges of cats demand tails without any evidence of knottiness, and a suggestion of kink in a cat's tail is in practice deemed a serious fault. The squint of the eyes (strabismus) is not mentioned in the English Standard at all, but both in theory and in practice crossed eyes in the Siamese is deemed intolerable. The squint is characteristic of the breed in its native country, the earlier importations manifested it, and it is still deemed to be an added virtue of the breed in China.

The English are recognized to be the greatest and most efficient breeders of livestock and to make over the various breeds they import into their own concepts and images. These made-over products are for the most part an improvement upon the materials they have to work with, both in the matters of utility and beauty. So it has been in the case of the Siamese cat. Neither crossed eyes or kinked tails are, in the analysis of their utility to a cat, desirable, and it is doubtful that they contribute to the animal's symmetry or beauty. Their elimination from the English version of the Siamese cat is entirely logical although it may detract from the ultimate interest in the variety.

It is to be regretted that we have been unable to trace the origin of the Siamese cat with a more categorical history. Other writers have speculated about that origin and have set their mere speculations down as findings. This we refuse to do. We are compelled to accept the Siamese cat as he is and to ignore where he may originally have come from. The fact is that nobody knows more than we have set down here. Stories of the provenience of the Siamese are, to put the matter mildly, merely apocryphal, not to label them fairy-tales. We can only guess.

21

C H I L D ' S   A P R O N
Resist-dyed cotton; Western China, 19th century
Lent by Dr. Carl Schuster

22

Something About Siam

HESE brief data about the country we recognize as the Kingdom of Siam—or as the Siamese choose to call it, Thailand—is not designed to throw any light upon the Siamese cat and the history of that variety of cat. It is rather intended to show that Siam has not been a static principality, and as a term, may embrace Burma, Cambodia, and almost the whole of the mainland of southeast Asia in addition to the territory now embraced in the present Kingdom of Siam. The Siamese cat may have had its origin in any part of that tremendous domain which from time to time has been under the aegis of the people known as the Thai.

Even now, Siam (or Thailand) is a country of vast extent. It is an area of approximately 200,000 square miles with a population, according to the last census in 1937, of some 14,500,000 persons. This area is equivalent to the combined areas of the American states of Maine, New Hampshire, Vermont, Massachusetts, Rhode Island, Connecticut, New York, New Jersey, Delaware, Maryland, Pennsylvania, and almost half of Ohio. Even this vast territory is a contraction of the larger extent of the country in former times, and it is entirely possible that the Siamese cat may have had its origin in what is now Cambodia, Burma, or Malaya (all three in part formerly included in the Kingdom of Siam), and yet be rightfully known as the Siamese cat. The census of 1937 probably shows an underestimate of the number of Siamese nationals. Any acquaintance with Siam and with its people will show us how nearly impossible it would be to canvass all of the vast numbers of primitive and outlying tribes that occupy the vast terrain, and any estimate of the population of Siam must remain a mere conjecture. We have enough to show us certainly that it is a vast country, numerously peopled. We can not ignore it as a small and obscure principality tucked away in an outlying corner of the universe.

The heart of Siam lies between Burma on its west and Indo-China on its east, within an amorphous outline that is roughly (very roughly) circular, and from that heart extends a tail or handle southward to include about two-thirds the length of the Malayan Peninsula. It occupies two-thirds the coastline of the Gulf of Siam, which is a large inlet from the South China Sea, and on the west side of the Malayan Peninsula impinges for more than a hundred miles upon the Bay of Bengal. The capital and largest city of the country is the royal city of Bangkok, otherwise known as Krungthep, with a population of 800,000 souls, situated on the banks of the Chao Phraya River, some twenty miles inland from where the river empties itself into the Gulf of Siam.

This vast metropolis of Bangkok, whose history goes back no further than the middle of the eighteenth century A.D., is the center of scholarship and the arts, the filter through which pass all goods and ideas received by the interior from the outside world, and the nucleus of the

24

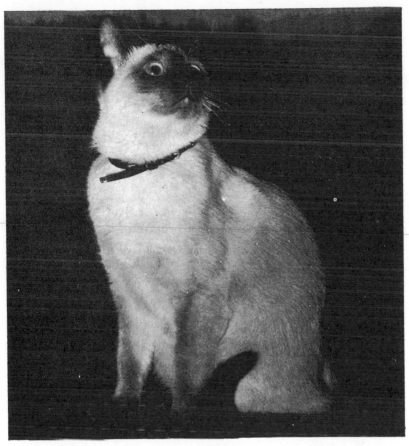

CONNIE

A member of the household of Mr. and Mrs. Roger Cohen,
Washington, D. C.

Photograph by Ernest P. Walker.

CABLE'S CROWN PRINCE, Blue Point Siamese Male Kitten
Sire: Dbl. Ch. Cable's Samarkand. Dam: Ch. Telot Cable.
Breeder-Owner: Mr. and Mrs. R. A. Cable, Blawnox, Pennsylvania.
This picture is being used on National Cat Week Seals in 1952.

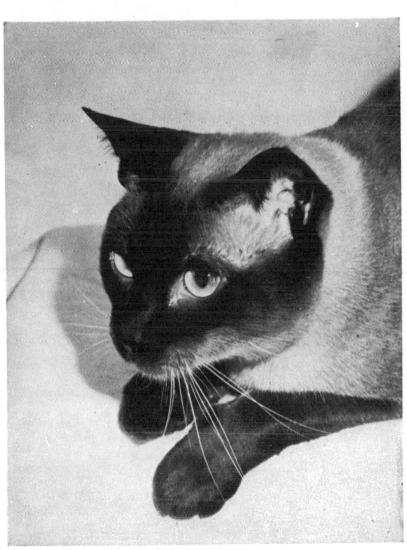

DOUBLE CHAMPION KNIGHT'S NICKLEBY
Owned by Mr. and Mrs. R. A. Cable, Blawnox, Pennsylvania.

NOR-MONT JADE
Breeder: Mrs. Merald E. Hoag.
Owner: Mr. and Mrs. Paul B. Gunnell, Jr., Silver Spring, Maryland.

highly centralized national government. It was from this city that is known to have come most of the Siamese cats exported to England and the Occident, and it may well have been in this city that the Siamese cat was first known or at least recognized as a distinct variety. Even yet, it is in the bazaars and shops of Bangkok that cross-eyed Siamese cats are occasionally offered for sale, although they do not compare in stamina and general excellence with cats obtainable in the western countries.

The whole of Siam lies between the Tropic of Cancer and the Equator and is subject to the typical monsoonal climate of southeastern Asia. In Northern, Central, and Eastern Siam there are three distinct seasons—the hot weather from February or March to May, the rains from June to October, and the so-called cold weather from November to February. When the northeast winds blow strongly, the cold weather is marked; but, at such times as the seasonal winds fail, the cold weather is scarcely distinguishable from the hot. In Northern Siam, which lies at greater distance from the sea and which possesses greater radiation, the days may be hot even during the cold season when the night temperatures afford a strong contrast by dropping as low as 50° F. and on the mountains even lower although never reaching freezing temperatures. The central plain, outside of Bangkok, is pleasantly cooled by the continuous sea winds, day and night; in Bangkok, however, perhaps because of houses of masonry instead of thatch and the drainage of surrounding marshes, the climate is appallingly hot and is said to be growing worse year by year. The peninsular area has the mildest and most equable climate, the greatest annual rainfall, and only two noticeable seasons—the hot weather from February to August and the rains from September to January, with the peak of the wet season occurring in December.

The Kingdom of Siam possesses a flora and fauna richer than that of most other areas of comparable size. The primitive jungles of the western and northern mountains show untrammeled nature at her tropical best. In the forests of these hills and valleys, high trees, bound to-

25

gether with vines, shelter such animals as the elephant, the tiger, and the gaur (a kind of wild ox), but so dense is the cover that the presence of large game is more often made known by signs than by actual sight. More than one thousand kinds of birds are known in the country, while fish of almost endless variety abound everywhere, from the Gulf of Siam to the smallest roadside ditches. The natural vegetation ranges from the most typically tropical plants to forms of the Temperate Zone, such as pines and violets, on the northwestern mountains. The peninsula, like the west and north, bears great forests rich in their species of animals and plants.

For an epitome of the history of Siam, we can do no better than to quote a paragraph from *Siam* by W. A. Graham, two volumes, published in London, 1924:

"From the earliest times the great peninsula which lies between India and China—has been peculiarly subject to foreign intrusion. Successive waves of Mongolian humanity have broken over it from the north, Dravidians from India have colonized it, Buddhist missions from Ceylon have penetrated it, and buccaneers from islands in the south have invaded it. Race has fought against race, tribe against tribe, and clan against clan. Predominate powers have arisen and declined. Civilizations have grown up, flourished and faded. And thus out of many and diverse elements a group of nations have been evolved, the individuals of which, Môn, Kambodian, Annamese, Burmese, Shan, Lao, Siamese and Malay, fundamentally much alike, but differing in many externals, have striven during centuries for mastery over each other, and incidentally over the countless minor tribes and clans maintaining a precarious existence in their midst. Into this mêlée of warring factions a new element intruded in the sixteenth century A.D. in the shape of European enterprise. Portuguese, Dutch, French and English all came and took part in the struggle, pushing and jostling with the best, until the two last, having come face to face, agreed to a cessa-

26

tion of strife and to a division of the disputed interests among the survivors. Of these there were but three, the French, the English, and the Siamese, and therefore Further India now finds herself divided, as was once all Gaul, into three parts. To the east lies the territory of French Indo-China, embracing the Annamese and Kambodian nations and a large section of the Lao; in the west the British Empire has absorbed the Môn, the Burmese and the Shans; while, wedged between and occupying the lower middle part of the subcontinent, with the isolated region of British Malaya on its extreme south border, lies the Kingdom of Siam, situated between 4°20′ and 20°15′ N. latitude, and between 96° 30′ and 106° East longitude."

The independence of Siam as a sovereign state, indeed, may be attributed to the jealousy and rivalry of the French and the British. Neither would permit the other to assume a predominant position in the country, either as a colony or a protectorate, and by playing off the one against the other, the Siamese have been able to maintain their independence, which, now with the British difficulties in Burma and Malaya and the French strife against the Viat Minh in Indo-China, appears to be secure and permanent.

Little is known about the first human occupants of Siam except some celts (a chisel or ax-shaped stone or metal implement employed by prehistoric and primitive peoples) from the Neolithic period found in the peninsula and on the eastern plateau. For all we know the users of these celts may have been preceded by even earlier races. In the mountains of the peninsula exist to this day small groups of dwarf, black-skinned, kinky-haired people, different from all other races in the country but closely related in type to the Andaman Islanders and the Negritos of the Philippines. It has been surmised that these Ngo (Semang) are the dwindling remnants of a once numerous population, successors to or descendants of the Neolithic man.

Following the Ngo and sometime during the past few millennia, it is believed there came successive waves of a people of Mongolian origin who drove the Negritos into the hills and settled in their place. These people are known as the Mon-Annam family and their descendants are the Môn (Peguans), the Cambodians, and the Annamese, as well as numerous semibarbarous lesser tribes which persist among the mountains.

After them, perhaps two or three thousand years ago, came another great population wave known as the Tibeto-Burman family, whence came the modern Burmese. They scarcely entered Siam at all at the time of their first invasion, but in comparatively recent times, driven from their homes by political disturbances, tribes of this stock migrated into Siam and Indo-China and were constantly reinforced by others of their blood brothers from the north.

The Mon-Annams and the Tibeto-Burmans were subsequently inundated by a third great family of migrants from the north, the Lao-Tai from the Yangtze Valley. This was a very strong and numerous people, for not only did they establish kingdoms far from their homeland, but also were a power in their own land and sought the mastery of all China. For centuries they waged successful wars upon their neighbors, but their propensity for wandering weakened their state and finally brought about its disintegration. The Chinese attacked them repeatedly, each attack producing a fresh exodus until, during the thirteenth century A.D., the Emperor Kublai Khan dealt them a final blow, crushing their power, and scattering them in all directions. Down the valleys of the Salwin and the McKhong Rivers came band after band of these Lao-Tai, in time intermingling and fusing with the Môn and Khmer stocks, resulting in the peoples which, since the founding of the city of Ayuthia, have been dominant in Siam. The principal divisions of the Lao-Tai family now living in the borders of Siam are the Thai (which means "free man"), the Siamese proper.

What is known about Siam prior to the fourteenth century of our era is rather obscure, being gleaned from a mish-mash of disconnected stories and fragments known as

"Pongsawadon Mu'ang Nu'a" ("Annals of the North Country"). From these annals, scholars have been able, by omitting the tales of the supernatural and highly improbable, to draw a rough picture of the condition of Siam at the dawn of historical time. Contemporary records of the period subsequent to the fourteenth century are available, the most important of them being "Pongsawadon Krung Kao" ("Annals of the Old Capitol" or "Annals of Ayutha"), which contains a complete and fairly accurate account of the history of Siam from 1349 to 1765. Since that latter date we have accounts of Siam by European travellers and missionaries.

The early thirteenth century saw the beginning of the last and greatest influx of Lao into the south of Siam. The victories of Kubla Khan over the Lao-Tai in southwest China drove many thousands of these people into northern Siam, where they upset the balance of power and caused the disruption of several states. As a result, many impoverished petty chieftains with their people turned south to seek new fortunes. During the following century, mingling with the Khmer and the Lao-Khmer, the Lao took over control from the earlier inhabitants and established capitals of their own, one of which, Supanburi, was in time to become dominant over all the others. When, at the middle of the fourteenth century, Phra Chao Uthong, King of Supanburi, marched westward to found a new capital, Nong Sano fell into his hands without a struggle and Uthong erected near it the new city of Maha Nakhon Si Ayuthaya (now known as Ayuthia), which was destined to become famous as the capital of one of the greatest kingdoms of Farther India.

Phra Chao Uhong (under the name of Phra Ramathibodi) became King of Ayuthia in 1359 and thereafter was occupied in bringing the outlying states and districts into line, in organizing his government, and in setting up a system of laws, parts of which continue in use up to the present time. The kingdom was theoretically the vassal of Cambodia; but, when the Cambodian king undertook to assert his rights as suzerain, Ramathibodi not only defeated him but pursued him well within the confines of his own country.

29

The kingdom continued to prosper under Ramathibodi's successors. During the next two centuries Buddhism definitely succeeded Brahamanism as the popular religion throughout the country. Great treasure was expended in beautifying the cities with graceful temples in the adopted Cambodian style which persists in Siam to this day.

In 1527, the King of Pegu, enraged by the exploits of Siamese marauders in one of his frontier provinces, collected an army and sent it into Siam under the leadership of his heir apparent, Bureng Naung. This prince defeated the Siamese in battle and besieged Ayuthia, itself. He met so stout a resistance in the long siege and his supply line so broke down that he was forced to give up and retreat to his own country, losing heavily in his rear guard actions all the way. After three years, Bureng Naung, having ascended the throne, took offense at the assumption of the title, "Lord of the White Elephants," again attacked Siam with a great army and again besieged Ayuthia, its capital. This time he was more successful and the Siamese King was compelled to negotiate with his conqueror and to turn over to him some of his white elephants, which had caused the difficulty. Just why the Siamese King's calling himself "Lord of the White Elephants" should so infuriate a rival king is not explained and is perhaps incomprehensible to the occidental mind.

Only a few years later the Siamese King undertook to repudiate Peguan suzerainty and Bureng Naung was on his neck again. The latter gained admission to Ayuthia through treachery, sacked and partially destroyed it, captured the King of Siam with many of his followers, and sent them in chains to Pegu. Leaving as his viceroy in Ayuthia the Siamese governor of Pitsanulok, Bureng Naung pressed on to subdue other cities but was scarcely out of sight when a Cambodian army, burning to revenge recent defeats and to reestablish ancient rights, appeared to begin a new siege of Ayuthia. This new enemy was repulsed but not before unprotected districts around the capital had been thoroughly looted.

Just now, when, attacked from east and west, her provinces despoiled and her people fugitive or captive, Ayuthia seemed doomed to early extinction, a hero arose to redeem her. This was Phra Naret, a son of Bureng Naung's viceroy. By his ability, bringing upon himself such a dislike by the Peguan King that his life was endangered, he revolted, about 1565, and led a Siamese army to sack and pillage Tenarrerim and Martaban. Two punitive expeditions sent against him were signally defeated, and Naret was crowned King of Siam. He at once began to restore Ayuthia and to repopulate it with captives brought from outlying districts which had attempted to cast off their allegiance.

Establishing his supremacy at home, Naret inflicted a crushing defeat upon another Burmese army, and then led a strong force against Cambodia. Th's campaign ended with the destruction of the Cambodian capital and the carrying of the King and many of his people captive to Ayuthia, where the king was executed. Finally, sometime about 1600, Naret invaded Burma with his great army, his object being to conquer the whole of that country. This project failed of its purpose, however, since Naret was killed in one of the early battles and his son and heir abandoned the enterprise and returned to his own dominions. Naret, within the space of about thirty-five years, had raised Siam from a condition of almost complete ruin to a position of ascendancy over all the neighboring kingdoms, and he left to his successors a great empire which was to endure for a period of 175 years.

During this period, Siam was becoming well known to European merchant adventurers trading in the Orient under the flags of Portugal, Holland, and England. The Malay Kingdom of Malacca had been conquered by the Portuguese early in the sixteenth century; individual Portuguese had reached A uthia and Pegu and had fought, some on one side and s me on the other, in the Siamo-Burmese wars; and Portuguese trading posts had been established in various Siamese ports. At the beginning of the seventeenth century, Portuguese missionaries arrived at Ayuthia, where they were well received and given lands for their churches.

At about this time, also, English and Dutch ships first appeared in Siamese waters and a bitter rivalry sprang up among the foreigners, who competed for commercial supremacy and the favor of the king, without which trade could scarcely be carried on at all. This struggle brought about endless quarrels and even desperate battles between the representatives of the rival powers, and by 1634 the Dutch had built a fortified factory at Amsterdam on the river Chao Phraya, carried on extensive commerce throughout Siam and monopolized the carrying trade to Japan and China. After the taking of Malacca by the Dutch in 1641, the influence of the Portuguese soon declined, although many of them continued to live in Siam, where some Portuguese family names survive among persons who display no evidences of European ancestry. The Dutch rapidly succeeded to all the commercial outposts of the Portuguese in Siam, devoting themselves chiefly to trade and taking little part in internal politics, except insofar as it affected their commercial prospects.

The first formal treaty contracted by Siam with any western power was entered into, in the year 1664, with the Dutch East India Company, authorized by the Dutch Republic. Dutch trade with Siam continued until 1706, when the royal favor was finally lost and the Company's agents were expelled from the kingdom.

In 1659 there arrived at Ayuthia one of the most extraordinary figures in the history of Siam. This was Constantine Phaulcon, the son of a Cephalonian innkeeper, who ran away on an English ship and, eventually making his way to Siam, stayed there to become Chief Minister to the crown and the trusted adviser to the King, Phra Naria. Under Phaulcon's guidance the country for a time prospered greatly. Not only were the Portuguese and Dutch traders, already established, encouraged to extend the scope of their enterprises but the English and the French East India Companies were invited to set up factories at the capital. The king in partnership with Phaulcon operated a fleet of trading vessels and became the principal trader of his own country.

ROMEO AND JULIETTE
The property of Mrs. Vary Campbell, England.

CHAMPION CHINDWIN'S SINGUMIN OF NEWTON
Fishing Horlick's Malted Milk Tablets out of the jar.
Owner: Mrs. Arthur C. Cobb, Newton, Massachusetts.

An illustration of crossed eyes, a fault which has been bred out in the Siamese.

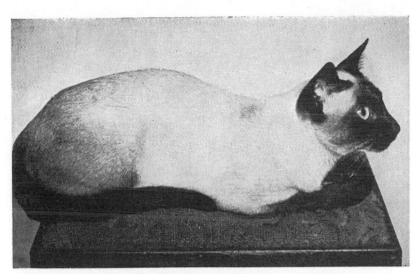

CHAMPION CHINDWIN'S SINGUMIN OF NEWTON
As a kitten won over 70 others at Empire Cat Club Show.
Best Siamese 5 times, Best Female in Show 4 times, in All Breed Shows.

NOR-MONT JADE   WHISKERS OF NOR-MONT
Breeder: Mrs. Merald E. Hoag.
Owners: Mr. and Mrs. Paul B. Gunnell, Jr., Silver Spring, Maryland.

"Si"
Owned by W. Margetson, England.

Tiam-O-Shian IV
Owned by Mrs. Vyvyan, England.

About this time it came to be believed in Europe that the whole of the Far East was ripe for conversion to Christianity and a Roman Catholic Mission was organized in France to put the project into effect. Ayuthia was considered the most central location for the effort, and in 1662 three French bishops with a staff of priests arrived there to inaugurate the work. Probably with the encouragement of Phaulcon, the bishops were favorably received by the king and made a considerable number of converts. They sought and obtained the support of Louis XIV, King of France, whose interests before long were centered upon more than the spiritual welfare of Siam; rather, instead, upon the economic interests of the Kingdom of France. A scheme was set afoot for the securing of the supremacy of France in the Asiatic kingdom through the agency of the priests, who believed that with the material support of the French King they should be able to convert to Christianity the Siamese monarch, himself. Six French warships and 1,400 French soldiers were sent to Siam, ostensibly to intimidate the Dutch, who were causing trouble from their fortress in Malacca. The two principal ports, Bangkok and Mergui, were garrisoned with a part of these French troops, and the King of Siam was induced to attach another part of them to his own person. The missionaries then began to exhort the king with all their eloquence but found that his conversion was more difficult than they had expected.

Their obstinate insistence with him and Phaulcon's ascendancy over him ended by alarming the Siamese, and a conspiracy among high officials of the Court succeeded in driving King Phra Narai from the throne, in killing Phaulcon, in expelling the European troops from the country, and in saving Siam from becoming the keystone of the great French empire in the Far East.

The Kingdom of Siam continued to prosper during several subsequent reigns marked with friendly relations with European nations, including the French, and a preoccupation with foreign commerce. However, in 1759, the Burmese initiated hostilities against the peace-loving Siamese and their attacks brought them to the very walls of Ayuthia.

The Burmese king sickened during this siege and died before he was able to retreat to his own country. Siam felt itself safe until 1766, in which year the Burmese attacked again and in the following year Ayuthia fell to the invaders and was given over to loot, fire, and rapine. The king escaped from the city, but was to die of exposure only a few days later.

The Burmese at that time were threatened by a Chinese invasion of Burma; and the Burmese king, Sin Byu Shin, leaving a viceroy and a small garrison to rule Siam, went home to repel the Chinese. Siam fell into anarchy; outlying districts set themselves up as independent; while robber bands preyed upon the people. A former official, Phraya Taksin, who had deserted the king at the time Ayuthia seemed likely to fall, by guile and treachery acquired complete authority in the southeast parts of the country and in due time appeared before the walls of Ayuthia as a national avenger. Overcoming the Burmese garrison and killing the viceroy, Taksin declared himself king and selected as his capital the village of Tonburi on the shore of Chao Phraya opposite the settlement of Bangkok, where a populous city soon came into being. He captured and murdered a legitimate pretender to the throne; and, with this last threat to his power removed, consolidated his government and made himself undisputed master of Siam.

However, Taksin's authority was to be short lived. He offended the nobility in various ways, while his excesses turned the people against him. In 1781, a cabal of courtiers proclaimed that Taksin was mad, dethroned him, and offered the crown to one of themselves, the son of a secretary to the last of the legitimate Kings of Siam. This nobleman, Phraya Chakkri, already popular, was readily accepted as king and ascended the throne in 1782, to found the dynasty that still reigns in Siam.

What is especially notable to us is that up to this point, no mention of the Siamese cat or of any cat appears in any history of Siam. Despite all the European contacts and explorations in the Far East, there is no record of any traveller's bringing back to Europe with him any unusual

34

cat, despite that the quest for novelties was unceasing and sailors are much given to bringing home with them unusual pets and animals they find in distant countries. It is impossible for us to affirm that the cat we know as the Siamese had not arisen and was non-existent up at least to the end of the eighteenth century, but it is remarkable that, if such cats were, none was brought to the West and no mention of their having been seen in the East occurs in any extant account written by any missionary, soldier, sailor, or trader in the Orient in that era. The story of the origin of the Siamese cat and the time of that origin is one that has never been unraveled and at this writing appears unlikely to be. It bids fair to remain a mystery.

Phraya Chakkri, who came to the throne of Siam as King Rama I and who founded the dynasty that has ruled the country continuously for 170 years, had scarcely assumed his new dignity when Bodaw Phra, King of Burma, attempted a new conquest of Siam. The Burmese were finally everywhere repulsed and defeated and, with the abandonment of Mergui and Tavoy by the Siamese in 1792, the recurrent wars between Siam and Burma had ended for good. The king was now at leisure to organize his government, the seat of which he transferred from Tonburi to Bangkok, on the left bank of the river, where he built a fortified city, which has been the country's capital to this day.

Rama II became involved in war at the very beginning of his reign. Cambodia had formally recognized the King of Siam as its suzerain and in 1786 had sent its infant king to be reared in Siam while meanwhile the Siamese rulers controlled the country. Annam, however, made identical claims to the suzerainty of Cambodia, and, when in 1809, the King of Annam sought to enforce his demands, an army was sent from Siam to combat his authority. A brief campaign ended with Rama's annexation of the Cambodian province of Phratabong, while the rest of the country became a dependency of Annam.

Upon the death of Rama II in 1825, the throne was usurped by a son of one of his lesser wives, while the legitimate heir, Chao Fa Mongkut, a young man of twenty-one, retired to the safety of the Buddhist monkhood. The reign of Rama III is chiefly notable for the resumption of political relations with the West. In 1833, a treaty drawn up between Siam and the United States of America represented the first formal tie between our country and any Asiatic power.

Chao Fa Mongkut, the half-brother of Rama III, had devoted himself as a monk to the study of English, the sciences, and the manners, customs, and governments of the West, at the same time missing no opportunity to meet and talk with European travellers. Coming to the throne at the death of Rama III in 1851, at the age of 47, he brought to his reign a remarkable enlightenment, which resulted in throwing Siam open to foreign trade and intercourse, in the introduction of such arts as printing and shipbuilding, in the construction of excellent roads and canals, in laying the foundations for systems of education and public health, and in numerous reforms directed toward increase of the public welfare. His love of learning was indirectly responsible for his death for, visiting a mountain peak to observe an eclipse in 1868, he contracted an illness from which he died in that year.

Rama IV's program of modernization was continued and expanded by his son, Rama V, the great Chulalongkou. Among the reforms instituted during his reign were the abolition of slavery for debt, the establishment of courts of law, the construction of railways, the spread of education, regulation of the conditions of military service, and radical changes in methods of revenue and rural administration. The appointment of trained officials under organized control in place of ignorant political governors and hereditary chieftains changed the country from a loose agglomeration of feudatory dependencies into the modern, homogeneous state.

What is of particular significance about Rama V to us is that it was in his reign that the first record of the exportation of Siamese cats to England occurred. It is alleged that the first of these cats and several subsequent ones were gifts of the king and of the royal family to English visitors in Siam, although such claims are difficult to authenticate.

It was also in this reign that difficulties with France occurred over the conflicting interests of the two countries in Cambodia. There were no bases for the French claims. Siam asked for a reasonable arbitration of the dispute, which was denied by the French. In 1893, bloody conflicts occurred which threatened to lead to war between Siam and France. Eventually Siam surrendered all of her territory east of the Me Khong River to France, including about half of the rich province of Luang Phrabong. As the French demands increased in numbers and severity, there was no longer any doubt that Siam's national survival was at stake. But, in 1896, Great Britain, at last alarmed by France's growing strength in southern Asia and unwilling to have her approach the eastern confines of India, intervened. Feelings in Britain and France ran high about the matter, but an agreement was concluded after lengthy negotiations, by which Siam's autonomy was guaranteed in order that she might serve as a buffer between the rival empires. Altogether in warding off her European neighbor on her east, Siam was compelled to sacrifice no less than 90,000 square miles of her eastern lands, which are now incorporated in the area we know as French Indo-China.

One of the last absolute monarchies, Siam in 1932 underwent a bloodless revolution. King Prajodhipok, a liberal, signed a new constitution, establishing a limited monarch, full franchise for the people, and an elected parliament. He refused to sign a measure taking away the royal power of life and death and resigned. He was succeeded by his nephew, Prince Ananda, a mere child born in 1925. King Ananda was found dead of a bullet wound on June 9, 1946, and the legislature named his brother, Prince Phumiphon Aduldet (born in 1928) to succeed him as king. Later

37

Parliament elected a two man regency to rule Siam for the new king.

It has never yet been definitely established whether the death of King Ananda was the result of suicide or murder. After a long trial, a palace servant, five years after the event, was convicted of his murder and now awaits execution for it. The verdict of murder, however, was established for political reasons; that it was just, remains doubtful.

A new Constitution, providing for a Senate and a House of Representatives elected by the people, was signed by King Ananda in 1946, and the first wholly elected Siamese Parliament was opened on June 1, 1946, just eight days before Ananda's death. It appears that the granting of this Constitution brought about the death of the king by murder or suicide, whichever it may have been.

Siam declared war upon the United States and Great Britain, January 25, 1942, under duress from the Japanese, but the king ruled August 16, 1945, that the declaration was void. The United States accepted the king's disavowal of the war, and a treaty ending the war was concluded with Great Britain, signed in Singapore, January 1, 1946.

Bangkok remains the chief city and metropolis of Siam. Here, in bewildering juxtaposition, the old Siam and the new confront the traveller on every side. The old is represented in the complicated network of canals, upon which thousands of boat-dwellers pass their lives; in the narrow streets hung with the vertical signboards of the inevitable multitude of Chinese traders; in the throngs of yellow-robed, Buddhist monks who appear at daybreak from hundreds of gaily colored shrines whose spires arise in all directions. The new is seen in the modern boulevards lined with spacious wooden houses set amid gardens and orchards; in the automobiles competing for space with bicycle-drawn jinrikishas; in the air-conditioned moving-picture theatres, where are shown the latest pictures shipped by air from Hollywood; in the various modern factories; in the great airport of Don Muang, north of the city, where transports arrive daily from Britain and Australia, from Java and The Netherlands.

Until recently, the inhabitants of towns and villages outside the capital lived a life not greatly different from that of their ancestors; one which revolved around the annual cycle of planting, growing, and the harvest, with religious festivals to break the monotony of living. Poverty, as understood in the industrial Occident, was unknown; for, while little actual money was seen by the average family in the course of a year, a house could be built of bamboo in a day or two. Fruit trees bore around the year; clothing was woven at home, and shoes were little worn; virtually everyone owned productive land or was at liberty to clear a tract from the forest which covers much of the thinly populated country; taxes were light and could be paid by a few days' labor on some project of public works.

During the decade of the thirties, the government had initiated a positive program aimed at raising the standards of living of the common people and especially of the peasants who constitute a large majority. Among the means adopted were the development of such new sources of gain as the raising of tobacco and cotton on a large scale; the construction of great irrigation projects and the development of sources of electric power; the education of the farmers in livestock breeding and scientific agriculture; the establishment of agencies to enable him to obtain a fair market for his produce; the spread of public health and medical services to the far corners of the provinces. This program was interrupted by the war, but it has since been resumed and is proving itself in the improvement of the conditions and the welfare of the people.

The prevailing religion is Buddhism. In 1939 there were 18,416 Buddhist temples and 140,774 priests, not to mention the innumerable yellow-frocked monks. Buddhism is a kindly, non-resistant religion, but one that, while not causing suffering, appears indifferent to it. A Buddhist may not kill an animal, but is under no religious obligation to alleviate its suffering or to prevent its death. The animals as well as many of the children, are hungry, bedraggled and neglected.

Some travellers declare that every inhabitant of Siam has a cat of some kind, but few foreigners have ever seen a Siamese cat in Siam. The cats are used to protect the granaries and houses from rats and mice which abound. Other travellers say that they saw no cats at all in the country, but this may be a mere failure of observation. The probable truth is something between these conflicting reports—that some Siamese, like some Americans, keep cats and that others do not. True Siamese cats, such as are in the West, recognized as members of that variety, are doubtless rare in Siam. This is not to be wondered at, since few breeds of livestock are kept pure and the color pattern of the Siamese cat, being a Mendelian recessive, is likely to be buried, even where the genes for it exist, under the dominant color patterns of other cats.

The Siamese Cat Comes to England and America

O MUCH buncombe has been said and written about the Siamese cat that it is difficult to make a categorical statement about the animal that will not be subjected to contradiction. This conflict of reports about it ranges from differences about the tempers and natures of the cats, their health and weaknesses, their prevalence and scarcity in Siam, whether they are a royal monopoly in Siam, their sacredness with the Buddhists, to all else about the breed. The fact remains that since its importation into England, the variety has been so much modified and "improved" that it is an English cat rather than Siamese.

There is a consensus of belief that the first of the Siamese cats to reach western shores were a pair brought from Siam by Owen Gould, at that time British Consul-General at Bangkok, in 1884. There is no record that Mr. Gould, himself, claimed that these two cats were a present, reluctantly made to him, by the King of Siam, but much romantic drivel has been printed about his difficulty in obtaining them. It seems more likely that they were merely purchased at some bazaar in Bangkok, like any other commodity. They later were given by Mr. Gould to his sister, a Mrs. Veley, and were exhibited by their owner at the Crystal Palace Cat Show the year following their importation. Mrs. Veley continued her interest in the variety and was one of the founders of the Siamese Cat Club in 1901.

Two years after this first importation, in 1886, a Mrs. Vyvyan imported two cats and two kittens from Siam into England. Mrs. Vyvyan and her sister, Miss Forestier Walker, were long to be among the foremost of the Siamese fanciers in England. Mr. Harrison Weir, the organizer and one of the judges at the first cat show held in England, mentions in his book about cats the Siamese of Lady Dorothy Nevill, whose cats were "imported and presented by Sir R. Herbert of the Colonial Office." Lady Marcus Beresford, who had a hand in everything pertaining to cats at the turn of the century, imported some Siamese, among which was a famous tom known as "The King of Siam." Two other imported inmates of Lady Marcus' famous cattery at Bishopsgate were "Tachin" and "Cambodia." These cats were all extensively bred from.

The then Duke of Wellington and a Mr. Scott of Rotherfield also imported Siamese cats into England, but there are no records of their cats ever having been bred from and the blood is presumed to have perished. There were doubtless other persons who from time to time brought cats from Siam, although these animals seem merely to have been pets and failed to find their way into the main blood-stream of the breed in England.

Therefore, we must conclude that the present strains of Siamese have been derived entirely from the crossing and intercrossing of the bloods of the imported cats of Mrs. Veley, Mrs. Vyvyan, Lady Dorothy Nevill, and Lady Marcus Beresford, at most an aggregate of eleven cats. This has of necessity entailed the frequent mating together of closely related cats and the interweaving and reinterweaving of the same source-blood within a single pedigree until the name of the same individual cat would appear thousands of times in the pedigree of any cat now alive if it were feasible to extend the pedigree to a sufficient length. That such intensive in-breeding as has been practiced in the Siamese cat has been carried out without harm to the variety (and in fact with positive good to it) is the best evidence we have that in-breeding, if judiciously practiced, is still our best method of perpetuating the type and increasing the vigor of Siamese cats.

All uniform breeds of domestic livestock have been derived from the breeding and subsequent in-breeding of a very few superior specimens, selecting the while the best for further breeding, and discarding the undesirable when it occurs. So far from being harmful to the breed, such a process not only improves the type but it also heightens the vigor of the race. Such a method the English genius for the breeding of pure races of livestock—and it is no less than genius—brought to the Siamese cat, altering it and bettering it to conform more nearly to the English concept of what the type should be. But it must be remembered that the English breeders employed what is altogether no more than perhaps eleven basic imported cats.

It would seem that the ancestors of all the Siamese cats in the United States came from Britain—all at least that were bred from. Among the earlier importers, it is possible to find only the name of Mrs. Clinton Locke of Chicago, who had Siamese about the turn of the century. It would appear that the impetus the breed has had in America came largely from that lady's activities in its behalf. There may have been other and even earlier importers, but their breeding programs seem to have come to naught. There have later been many importations of Siamese cats from Britain, and from these the cult of the Siamese cat had its inception in the United States.

43

Merchant sailors were wont to bring into the port of San Francisco in the nineties many weird animals from the orient, Chow-Chow dogs from China, sun-bears from Malaya, pythons and anacondas from the Philippines and from India, monkeys, lizards and gaudily feathered birds from the far parts of the earth. These they would sell for whatever they would bring. Among this miscellany are reported to have been "cross-eyed monkey-cats," which could have been only Siamese or some derivative of that variety. The sailors alleged, and probably believed, that such cats were the result of the cross between a monkey and a cat, which we recognize to be preposterous despite that the Siamese evinces in his nature a monkeyesque temperament and disposition which may well have inspired the concept of such hybridization. The cat fancy on the West Coast early in the century was devoted almost entirely to the Siamese to the exclusion of other varieties of cats. There is, however, no reason for belief that the "cross-eyed monkey-cats" brought in by the sailors and sold as novelties were ever bred from. Most of them were frail (as were the Siamese imported into England) and were subsequently neglected and uncared for. We are unable to consider these "cross-eyed monkey-cats" as a contribution to the blood-stream of the Siamese cat as we know the variety in America and England.

The Siamese Cat in Other Countries

Siamese predominate in the South African Cat Fancy, although a great number of them are hybrid. Many of these specimens are black-coated, with blue eyes typical of the breed. At a show held by the Western Province Cat Club, Siamese prevailed over the other exhibits to the extent of thirty-one out of a total of fifty-four. The prize for the best exhibit in the show was awarded to Momchao Phaun, a cat actually bred by the King of Siam himself and owned by Mrs. Bendyshe Walton of Grahamstown. Another winner was the Siamese kitten, Sebastian Periwinkle of Brakkekloof, owned by Miss F. Pocock, Chairman of the South African Cat Union.

Owing to the beautiful climate in South Africa, shows are

usually held in the open air. Cats are not penned as in Britain and the U.S.A., but sit in collar and lead and watch the proceedings, or in the arms of their owners. Here is an extract from South African show rules: "Every exhibit should have a comfortable basket, car, or lap in which to sit during the show and be seen by the public. The owner must accompany the exhibit and be in the judging room during the judging for the class entered, and must carry the exhibit to the judges' table when required."

The Siamese Fancy in Australia is not as yet of any considerable size, but interest is rapidly increasing. Special enthusiasm appears to be shown for seal-pointed cats; the blue-pointed variety are at present almost unknown. However, one or two ardent breeders are importing them from Britain. At a show held in Melbourne, twelve Siamese cats were exhibited, and created so much interest that enthusiasts decided to organize a special club for the breed, with the result that the Siamese Cat Club of Australia was born. This club models its rules as closely as possible on the British Siamese Cat Club, and it works to raise the standards of Siamese cats in its own country.

On the Continent, Siamese cats are very popular indeed, although at present the standard is not considered to be as high as in Britain. Short, kinked tails appear to be a special feature, and in describing one of the exhibits for her report of the Cat Club de Paris Show in 1949, our own eminent judge, Mrs. Joan Thompson, wrote: "This fault I found in nearly every exhibit, and some of the tails brought memories of the Siamese as they were in England when I first commenced to handle them as a steward over twenty years ago."

And, again, in reporting on the International Cat Show at San Pellegrino, July 1948, Marcel Reney has written: "In Siamese the males were better than the females, but the heads were too round, and the colour too dark; several had beautiful blue eyes. They bear out what I have written in my book, *Nos amis les Chats*, that the exhibitors on the Continent should import several good specimens from England to get back the standard of the beautiful Siamese."

'Virtue preserved from fell destruction's blast.'

*Pericle*s. V. 3.80

Judging the Siamese Cat

AT shows, though even more numerous and larger in Britain, have come to be recognized and anticipated by the public in many of the larger and some of the smaller American cities. Intended, as they are, to further an appreciation and the well-being of cats of various varieties, they also serve a further purpose, notably the promoting of a standardization and uniformity of the breeds which will discourage mongrelism and "alley-cattery." The various breeds are classified and judged in the order of their excellence by presumed experts with long knowledge and experience with cats of the various breeds.

How, it may be asked, may a cat be judged? The answer is that each breed has a written standard of excellence which describes and prescribes perfection for the variety in question. These standards of excellence must needs be brief; from them are omitted many of the qualifications that judges are presumed to know; and in them are often included specifications that make tolerable some undesirable attributes.

If the Standard for the Siamese cat were fully explicit and correct, this chapter would be supererogatory and might well be omitted from this book. However, there are many owners of Siamese cats, who, without any aspirations to become judges, wish to pass upon and assess the merits of their own cats and who are balked by the terms set forth in the Standard. This is intended to elucidate the Siamese Standard and not to quarrel with its specifications; in anything said here that appears to be at variance with the Standard, the Standard must supercede these remarks and must govern.

Let it be said here that, except the matter of soundness, which the Standard takes for granted and says nothing about, the excellence or failing of a Siamese cat is purely arbitrary. If a cat is satisfactory to his owner who can find no fault with him, if the cat fills the owner's eye and stimulates in him an aesthetic appreciation, if he is the kind of cat, in short, that the owner wants, who is to say that he is not a good cat, whatever he may look like? That is the cause of the greatest dissatisfactions with the showing and judging of cats. An owner whose cat fails to win in a cat show is prone to feel that his own cat is a veritable paragon of perfection and that all the other cats are inferior in all respects in which they fail to look exactly like his. All the cats are out of step but Tommy.

Such an attitude is well enough for the owner's private admiration. We should all be loyal to our particular animals. However, there exists a standard of uniformity which defines a breed, and an approximation to that uniformity is all that determines a cat's membership in his own variety, however he may be bred. Judges of cats are not infallible, and some of them may even be venal; but the position of a cat in the list of awards, while not final, is at least indicative of his comparative general merits.

The Siamese tends to controvert all the canons of cat structure. Quite aside from its unusual markings of

48

LADY MARCUS BERESFORD
From a painting by Edward Hughes.

LITTER OF SIAMESE KITTENS
Belonging to Lady Marcus Beresford.

SIAMESE KITTENS
Sire: Zeke Deke. Mother: Kopper Lustre.
Owner: Mrs. A. E. Albera, Denver, Colorado.

CHAMPION HOLLYWOOD BLUE VELVET
Blue Point Siamese Female, owned by E. W. Krampert of
Casper, Wyoming.

CABLE'S FIGALETTE, Seal Point Female
Sire: Dbl. Ch. Knight's Nickleby. Dam: Newton's Figa.
Breeder-Owner: Mr. and Mrs. R. A. Cable, Blawnox, Pennsylvania.

NUNKY
A member of the household of Mr. and Mrs. Walter C. Kackley,
Washington, D. C.
Photograph by Ernest P. Walker.

GRAND AND DOUBLE CHAMPION CYMRI DEE-VA
Sired by Ch. Cymri Cri-ket
Made her points for Grand Ch. in less than three months, believed to
be the World's Record.
Breeder-Owner: Mrs. Lillian E. Pedulla, Norristown, Pa.

"points," the Siamese is different from other cats in many particulars, as different, in fact, as a Thoroughbred horse is different from a Percheron, and in much the same fashion. The Siamese is the Thoroughbred of the tribe of domestic cats.

The Siamese is a comparatively small cat and lightly made throughout, as opposed to the cart-horse bone that is desirable in other cats. He is higher at his pelvis than at his withers, whereas in most cats a levelness in backline is desirable. The Siamese has a long, tapering, finely made tail, as against the short, thick, heavily made tail wanted in other cats. His skull is comparatively narrower than those of other breeds of cats; his face and muzzle longer, without being weak or pinched; his blue eyes set obliquely in his head. All this is different from the heavy, round skull, the short muzzle, and the forward looking eyes of the ordinary cat. However perfect his "points" and color may be as a Siamese, a cat is not a true Siamese if he had the short, broad, round head we look for in other breeds of cats. We shall return more explicitly to these various features as we go along.

Marking and points are of course necessary on a Siamese, and a cat can not be called a Siamese at all without an approximation to the correct color pattern. However, that is no more important than the characteristic structure, the make and shape, that we have learned to associate with the pattern. How often do we see a big, clumsy, lummox of a cat with Siamese color, markings and points lolling in a cage at a show and classified as a Siamese solely upon the basis of his pattern. Such a cat has small chance of winning under a judge who knows his business. Rather a good judge will sacrifice something in the matter of markings and go instead for a cat of better structure and a degree of mediocrity in pattern.

But the true Siamese must have both—good markings on a correctly made cat. Neither can be omitted. And soundness! Too few judges of cats pay sufficient attention to soundness, and this is particularly true in the Siamese. It is true that, in the earlier days of the Siamese cat in England, the breed had a reputation of being frail and difficult to rear, which was probably owing to the fact that the cats at that time imported from Siam and bred from were unsound. The thoroughly sound Siamese is as hardy as any other cat, as difficult to kill, and endowed with the proverbial nine lives. This hardihood has been brought about by the constant and unintermittent selection of sound breeding stock on the part of British breeders, and it should not be overlooked by the judges. Of course, it is impossible for a judge to assess the internal economy and constitutional vigor of an exhibit within the short time at his disposal, but lack of vigor is often reflected in the state of the coat, the expression of the eyes, and above all in an unsteady stance or gait of an animal under examination.

Let us first consider the Siamese cat as a complete entity, after which we shall proceed to its parts.

The Siamese is a small cat, somewhat smaller all over than most of the other varieties. Size is no virtue. Big Siamese are prone to be coarse and ungainly, lacking the "svelt" appearance, the lissomeness that is so characteristic of the breed as a whole. In fact, a Siamese of excessive size is open to the suspicion that it is not purebred and that it may harbor some blood of some other variety. Neither may excessive smallness be considered a virtue, although it is not a fault. A Siamese may be as small as you will, but a small cat just because of its lack of size should not be placed over one of moderate size.

In Siam there is said to exist a large variety of the Siamese cat, but occidentals are not known ever to have see a specimen of the variety, and it is open to doubt that it exists at all.

In station the Siamese is somewhat tall—that is he is a little more on the leg than western cats. This is not to say that he should be leggy or giraffe-like, but only that he should show a little more daylight under him than the other cats. While this is true in fact, there is about him an illusion of height of station which is due to the shortness and closeness of his coat, which is even shorter than the other short-haired cats.

50

In the matter of bone and substance, the Siamese carries only a moderate amount—enough that his bone-structure does not appear delicate but not so much as to cause him to be or to appear clumsy. In the occidental cats, the judges are prone to demand and look for all the bone structure they are able to find, but in this respect the Siamese is different. The Siamese is the Thoroughbred and not the cart-horse of the cat family. His moderate amount of bone is hard and strong, never spongy and never with any symptoms of rickets or indication that he has ever had that disease of the bones or joints. We are compelled to remember the word "svelt" as it appears in the Standard and to realize that any excess of bone over the amount needed to sustain the animal in his wild activity detracts from the sveltness of his lines and hampers him in his speed and lissomeness.

The Siamese is higher behind than at the shoulder; his back-line is up-grade from the withers to the pelvis, whereas in most other cats a level or horizontal top-line is demanded. This means that the hind-legs of the Siamese are longer than the fore-legs. This aspect is attained not by the straightness of the hind-legs, which would cause the cat to appear prop-like and ungainly, but rather by their actual length. There is considerable turn to the stifles and hocks, which enables the cat to propel himself with rapidity, to crouch, and to spring with power. The hams should be large, hard and powerful, but not so prominent as to impair the aspect of activity.

In the critical evaluation of any quadruped, it is to be remembered that the animal's power of movement has its origin in its hind-legs, which must be well angulated and sturdy, and that this power is transmitted through the spine and muscles of the back to the forehand. No power is developed in the front part of the cat, but the shoulders and fore-legs serve only as a point of suspension to keep the animal from tumbling forward upon its face.

This is not to say that the shoulders and their placement play no part in the animal's action. A straight, proppy shoulder, with an upright scapula which is not well angulated

51

with the humerus, impedes the cat's agility and destroys its efficiency, besides reducing the length of neck and the appearance of grace. A well laid-back shoulder, on the other hand, opens to permit the cat to take a long forward stride, a stride long enough to accommodate and utilize the power transmitted through the back from the hindquarters. Nothing is more awkward appearing than a cat with shoulders so forward placed as to waste its power and unable to keep up in front with the long strides in the rear which come from well bent and powerfully used stifles and hocks.

The Siamese is not fundamentally a short cat, such as the other varieties are. His body is long enough for him to display sinuosity and lissomeness, but not so long as to exhibit any slackness of spine or loss of power. His body is at all times in command of itself, but without stiffness or constriction.

The arms are dead straight from elbows to feet, with only a moderate amount of bone. The important thing is that the elbows shall not be loose or the shoulders tied. Standing or moving, the fore-legs are parallel, neither truss-legged with the feet further apart than the elbows nor an inverted triangle with the feet together. In movement the legs should swing freely and directly forward. The pastern joint should be straight or almost nearly straight, with no sign of softness or weakness.

The feet are, of course, small, short, deep, and compact. The retractile claws need no shortening, except for the cat's access to a scratching board, upon which he will keep his claws in shape while he takes his calisthenics as he tenses his muscles and stretches the ligaments of his joints.

The structure of the Siamese skull differs markedly from that of other cats, also. The top-skull, without being narrow, is not wide and it slopes noticeably from the brow to the occiput. The top-skulls of other cats are as wide and rounded across as is possible. The foreface of the Siamese is moderately long, but not weak or snippy. In the occidental varieties of cats, the demand is for a short wide muzzle, which is quite foreign to the Siamese. Indeed, nothing makes one more suspicious that a Siamese is attenuated with the blood of some other variety of cat than the broad skull and the short muzzle.

Of the mouth of the Siamese we need take little cognizance except to make sure that the teeth are clean, white and not diseased. The feline occlusion is seldom faulty, and there is no occasion to examine it unless some malformation is apparent when the mouth is fully closed. The cat has 32 teeth which (barring accident or old age) are usually all present. On the whole, the mouth and teeth of the Siamese present little difficulty.

The eyes of the Siamese are not exactly round, but rather of the shape of a short, fat almond. They set somewhat obliquely in the skull, whose formation offers the accommodation. The Siamese eyes should never be round and set directly forward under the brow as in other kinds of cats; in the correctly formed skull, it is impossible for this to occur.

In the occidental version of the Siamese cat, the squint or strabismus of the eyes is a major fault, despite its value in the cat's native land and throughout the East, where it is deemed not only weird and interesting but characteristic of the breed. Doubtless the animal's vision is somewhat impaired by crossed eyes, which is equally doubtless the reason why the British breeders have declared such a feature undesirable and have sought to breed it out of the stock. This they have well nigh succeeded in doing, and an official judge of the breed has no discretion but to penalize the fault severely. In the Siamese that is not intended for exhibition, crossed eyes may be considered as an added virtue and, in view of their being an essential of the breed in Siam, cannot be considered as foreign to it. However, one is ill-advised to exhibit a Siamese with a squint in an occidental cat show.

In extreme excitement or intense interest, it is rare to find a Siamese that does not exhibit some degree of strabismus. This is to be forgiven and is not subject to penalty because it is so general as to be all but universal.

The color of the eyes of the Siamese is an agate blue of as deep a shade as it is possible to find. It is seldom intense but on no account should it be light, watery, or washed out. It is said that the Siamese eyes turn red or show red glints in the dark and under artificial illumination. This phenomenon pertains only to the pupils which alternate in certain artificial lights between black and a dark ruby color, and many persons familiar with the Siamese fail to see the ruby-like glints. It is at best immaterial, because cats are not judged in the dark.

The ears of the Siamese are of normal length with broad bases set firmly on the head. Unless they are obviously anomalous, their structure and placement may be taken for granted to be correct.

The tail of the Siamese is somewhat thinner and longer than that of other cats, but is heavier at its insertion into the spine than midway in its length. The tail is for a cat both a rudder and a balancing device. It is probably for the reason of its greater efficiency as a rudder that the logical British have put a practical ban on kinks in the tail, which like squinted eyes, are desiderata in the far East. It is true that the Standard gives lip-service to the toleration of the kinked tail, but in actual judging of the Siamese a kinked tail is considered to be a fault and is seldom tolerated.

The Siamese must stand firmly and gracefully upon all four legs, the front legs parallel to each other and to the hocks; he must move forward without signs of weakness or of being crippled. The hocks must not turn inward (cow hocks) or outward (bandy legs). Above all must we be quick to observe signs of present or former rickets, which manifest themselves in bent bones, enlarged joints, clumsy or crippled movement, or bowed quarters.

The structure of the Siamese cat is discussed here in such length and detail because it is primary in the evaluation of that cat. However excellent the color, markings and pattern upon a Siamese may be, he can not be a typical specimen unless he be as well made as he is marked. It is to be feared that too many judges overlook structure and soundness of the cat in favor of a beautiful pattern. Both are so important as to be essential, but the structure must come first. It is like an edifice, which must be well built on a sound foundation before its decorations are of any worth.

The standard of perfection as drawn up and adopted by the Siamese Cat Club (of England) offers a tacit admission that structure is even more important than marking in that it allows but 10 points for body color and 10 points for "points" (or markings) in its scale of one hundred points for the entire cat. The citation here of the scale of points found in the Standard is not to be accepted as a brief for score-card judging. The comparison system is much to be preferred. The scale of points is cited merely to show the emphasis put upon structure as compared to color and markings by the Siamese Cat Club.

This is not to say that good markings are to be ignored on a good cat. They are a *sine qua non,* and a Siamese without at least adequate markings is not a Siamese at all.

There are three recognized colors—the seal-pointed, the rarer blue-pointed, and the rarest chocolate-pointed. In pattern all are alike, the difference being merely in colors. The seal-pointed is most prevalent and best known, the popularly recognized Siamese, and therefore most fit for somewhat lengthy discussion.

The body color of the seal-pointed is cream, a very rich cream, shading gradually into a light fawn, especially on the back. The exact color beggars description, but this is as specific as the color can be made. The kittens are white all over at the time of their birth and deepen into cream and fawn on their body somewhat later. This process does not stop with their maturity but continues until, after two or three years of age, a Siamese is likely to be too dark for exhibition. Some judges make allowance for this darkening process in cats past their full maturity and attach no penalty to it. This is to be encouraged, since otherwise the exhibition life of a truly great cat may be confined to the period between his first and second birthdays. An old

55

cat too dark for exhibition is none the less as good for breeding purposes as he was before he began to darken.

The "points" in the seal-pointed variety are of a rich, dark, seal brown verging upon black. The standard declares that the points are "clearly defined," which is a desideratum impossible of attainment. In fact, it should read "defined as clearly as it is possible to have them." In real life the seal shades gradually into the body-color and mingles with it at the margins of the markings. The feet are seal which extends part way up the legs, almost or quite to the elbows. The rear feet and hocks are seal with considerable shading of seal into the body-color over the quarters. The tail is distinctly seal. The ears are seal except for some lighter hairs on their insides. The entire mask is seal, which extends upward to include the brow and backward over the forehead. Traces of seal extend from the mask to the ears with the maturity of the cat. In kittens all the markings are scanty and are not to be anticipated to be complete before they are a year old. In kittens the feet are brown only to the pastern joint, the mask does not extend beyond the eyes, and the traces from mask to ears is undeveloped. A kitten with the full markings of an adult cat may be expected to be too dark all over with its maturity.

The blue-pointed Siamese, much less numerous than the seal-pointed cats, is exactly like the seal-point, except in its color. This color is icy, light bluish white on the body, with all the points a darker shade of glacial blue. These points are in exactly the same areas as the heavier marking on the seal-pointed cat. The body coat darkens with age as in the seal-point and the kittens before their maturity are not fully marked.

The chocolate-pointed cat, once very rare is now becoming more numerous year by year. The body-color is ivory, suffused later in life with light chocolate. The points, in the same areas as in the other two varieties, are rich milk chocolate, much lighter than the color of bitter chocolate. The tendency of the ears to be darker than the other points is to be discouraged. The most recent color

A LITTER OF KITTENS FROM CHIRN-SA-HAI-SO-MAI
Owner: Mrs. L. L. Lessard, Minneapolis, Minnesota.

GRAND CHAMPION NEWTON'S JAY TEE
The first Seal Pointed Grand Champion.
Photograph taken a month before her death at 10 years, in October, 1951,
but her picture is still of interest. A particularly nice one as it
shows her sweet expression.
Owner: Mrs. Arthur C. Cobb, Newton, Massachusetts.

CHIRN-SA-HAI-SO-MAI, Seal Point Siamese Female
Sire: Dbl. Ch. Cha-Wa-Chirn-Sa-Hai.   Dam: Sun Yee of Chirn-Sa-Hai.
Breeder: Mrs. R. L. O'Donovan, Chirn-Sa-Hai Cattery, South Miami,
Florida.
Owner: Mrs. L. L. Lessard, Minneapolis, Minnesota.

CABLE'S SARITA	CABLE'S HY-KEE
Shaded Silver Persian Female	Blue Point Siamese Female
Sire. Dbl. Ch. Babe LeRoy of	Sire: Dbl. Ch. Knight's Nickleby
Beverly Serrauv	Dam: Ch. Par-Ami Cho Cho San
Dam: Silver Lady Fair	

Breeder-Owner: Mr. and Mrs. R. A. Cable, Blawnox, Pennsylvania.

SIAMESE KITTENS
Bred and owned by Mr. and Mrs. L. R. Van Riper, Rockville, Maryland.

TWO SEAL POINT, ONE BLUE POINT SIAMESE
Owned by Mr. and Mrs. Paul B. Gunnell, Silver Spring, Maryland.

IMPORTED ORIENTAL NANKI POOH OF NEWTON

Before his death, Nanki Pooh held the record in America for the most off-
spring who made their championships. He sired over 1,000 kittens.

Owner: Mrs. Arthur C. Cobb, Newton, Mass.

NOR-MONT JADE   WHISKERS OF NOR-MONT

Breeder: Mrs. Merald E. Hoag, Arlington, Virginia.

Owner: Mr. and Mrs. Paul B. Gunnell, Jr., Silver Spring, Maryland.

addition is the lilac point. As time goes by, perhaps other colors will be developed by imaginative breeders.

The coat, the same in all varieties except in the colors as noted, is dense, short, fine, glossy in health, and close lying. The density manifests itself in a sort of protective wooliness through which the guard-hairs of the short outer coat protrude. Except for its shortness and tendency to softness, the coat of the Siamese is little different from the coat of other short-haired cats.

The foregoing is a description of the ideal in the Siamese cat. It will be found in practice that no specimen entirely fulfills the specifications of the ideal. While perfection may never be fully realized, the idea is something toward which we may breed our cats.

Official Standard of the Siamese Cat

National Siamese Cat Club

Judge's Score

Color 25
Coat 10
Condition 5
Head (including eye set) 20
Type (including shape, size and
    sveltness) 20
Color and shape of eyes 20

COLOR: Siamese cats shall be known as Seal Points, Blue Points, Chocolate Points, and Lilac Points.

BODY COLOR: In judging older cats, allowances should be made for darker coats, since Siamese generally darken with age, but there should be a definite contrast between body color and points. Point allotment: Proper color, 4; proper shading, 4; evenness of color, 7; Kittens, lighter in color.

POINTS: Mask, ears, legs, feet and tail, dense and clearly defined, all of the same shade. Mask should be connected to the ears by tracings except in kittens. Point allotment: Mask, 2; ears, 2; legs, 2; feet, 2; tail, 2.

COAT: Short, fine in texture, glossy, lying close to the body.

Point allotment: Short coat, 3; fine coat, 2; glossy coat, 2; close coat, 3.

CONDITION: Good physical condition, not fat, inclined to muscle. Judges to penalize for emaciation.

HEAD: Head should be long and should taper in a fine wedge from ears to narrow muzzle, with no whisker break. The receding chin caused by failure of the upper and lower teeth to meet in a straight line shall be considered a serious fault. The skull is to be flat, and the nose is to be a continuation of the forehead with no break. In profile, a straight line is to be seen from the center of the forehead to the tip of the nose. Allowance is to be made for jowls in a stud cat. There should be the width of an eye between the eyes. Ears rather large and pricked wide at the base and should continue the line of the wedge. Allotment of points: Long flat profile, 6; fine muzzle, 4; non-receding chin, 4; width between the eyes, 2; ears, 4.

BODY TYPE: The body should be medium in size, dainty, long and svelt. Males should be proportionately larger than females. Neck long and slender. Legs proportionately long and slim; hind legs slightly higher than the front. Feet small and oval in shape. Tail long and tapering with no visible kinks. Point allotment: Body, 7; neck, 4; legs and feet, 5; tail, 4.

EYES: Eye aperture almond shape and slanting toward the nose in true Oriental fashion. Point allotment: Color, 10 (clear, 5; deep blue, 5); shape, 10 (Oriental, 5; uncrossed, 5).

UNDESIRABLE FOR ALL SIAMESE: Rounded head, fat, thick set specimens. Hood (a continuation or an extension of the point coloring over the top of the head, around the sides and under the throat. The mask, instead of fading away gradually at the throat makes a distinct change in color so it would appear that a hood was tied around the head. Tracings to the ears are lost as the mask continues up between the ears). Rough shaggy coats. Odd eye color; grey or yellowish tinge in eyes, crossed eyes. Belly and hip spots. Tabby or ticked markings. Light hairs in the points. White feet or toes. Receding chin. Invisible kink.

58

SEAL POINT SIAMESE: Color: even pale fawn to cream, shading gradually into a lighter color on the stomach and chest. The coat color should not be grey. Points all the same shade of deep seal brown. Eyes shall be clear and of a vivid deep blue color. Footpads and nose leather the same color as the points.

BLUE POINT SIAMESE: Coat color is to be a bluish white changing gradually to an oyster white on the stomach and chest. Points should be all the same shade of definite blue giving strong contrast of divided color. There must be no fawn in the coat. Foot pads and nose leather to be slate colored. Eyes clear and as deep blue as possible within the breed.

CHOCOLATE POINT SIAMESE: Body color ivory all over. Points milk chocolate color. Grey or dingy shading on the body is a fault. Foot pads and nose leather a cinnamon pink color. Eyes clear and as deep blue as possible within the breed. Pale or slatey eyes to be discouraged.

LILAC POINT SIAMESE: Body color to be glacial white. Points, frosty grey with pinkish tone. Foot pads and nose leather mauve. Eye color clear and as deep blue as possible for the breed. Pale or slatey eyes to be discouraged.

The Official Standard of the Siamese in Great Britain

adopted by the Governing Council of the Cat Fancy

THE SEAL-POINTED CAT

SCALE

TYPE AND SHAPE 50
Head 15—Ears 5—Eyes 5—Body 15—Legs
and Paws 5—Tail 5

Medium in size, body long and svelte, legs proportionately slim, hind legs slightly higher than front ones, feet small and oval, tail long and tapering (either straight or slightly kinked at the extremity). Head long and well proportioned, with width between the eyes, narrowing in perfectly straight lines to a fine muzzle, giving the impression of a marten face. Ears, rather large and pricked, wide at the base.

COLOUR 50

EYES 15: Clear, bright and decidedly blue. Shape oriental and slanting towards the nose. No tendency to squint.
BODY COLOUR 10: Cream, shading gradually into pale warm fawn on the back. Kittens paler in colour.
POINTS 10: Mask, ears, legs, feet and tail dense and clearly defined seal brown. Mask complete, and (except in kittens) connected by tracings with the ears.
TEXTURE OF COAT 10—CONDITION 5: Very short and fine in texture, glossy and close lying.

TOTAL 100

THE BLUE-POINTED CAT

Same as above, with following exceptions:
BODY COLOUR: Glacial white, shading gradually into blue on back, the same cold tone as the points, but of a lighter shade.
EYE COLOUR: Clear, bright china blue.

THE CHOCOLATE-POINTED CAT

TYPE: Same as for seal-pointed cat.
COLOUR POINTS: Milk-chocolate colour, the ears, mask, legs, paws and tail to be as even in colour as possible, the ears should not be darker than the points.
EYES: A good china blue (pale slaty eyes to be discouraged).
BODY COLOUR: Ivory colour all over. Shading, if at all, to be the colour of the points. Grey or dingy shading will be a fault.
TEXTURE: As for seal-pointed cat.
CONDITION: As for seal points.

The Character of the Siamese Cat

T HAS been alleged by many persons that the Siamese cat is more like a dog in his nature than like other cats. This can well be denied. While he is in some minor respects different from other cats, he remains essentially what he is, a cat with all the feline attributes. His resemblance to a dog is predicated upon a greater intelligence than other cats possess, but there is some doubt that dogs are smarter than cats. Moreover, the Siamese is more fond of human companionship than other cats, which causes some persons to compare him to a dog; but the Siamese is not dependent upon humans, as the dog is. He is quite capable of fending for himself. He attaches himself to persons for love of company and for what he can get out of them.

The Siamese is an inveterate beggar and insists upon having what he has set his heart upon, whether it is food, being let out or turned in, or a certain chair upon which he chooses to lie. But quite as much as having his wants satisfied, the Siamese likes to converse with a human. As long as he is talked to, hours at a stretch, he will respond with an inflected meow that appears like an effort to speak.

Quite aside from conversation, however, the Siamese is an infernally noisy cat. Even alone or with other cats, his incessant meowing keeps up, even at the times that he wants nothing and is fully satisfied. The persistence of his chatter is very annoying to some persons, who are all but driven mad by it. It is one of the unpleasant things, perhaps the most unpleasant, about Siamese nature.

This is especially true of the "calling" of the Siamese queen (or female) at the time of her oestrum or heat. The calling of the queens of other varieties of cats may reach a degree of intensity, but not so great as that of the Siamese. It is in line with her begging for anything that she may want, and in this case it is her begging for permission to go out in search of a mate. It is the family yowling raised to the nth power. It is not only intense, loud, interminable, and persistent, but hysterical. It may, if not gratified, lead to convulsions. It may be deemed better to permit her to find a mongrel mate—even if kittens are not wanted—than to endure her frustration and her pleading to get out. This performance is likely to be repeated each time that the queen comes into heat, but is not likely to be so hysterically intense after she has had one litter of kittens.

The only method by which she can be quieted is by spaying, by which is meant the removal of her ovaries. This surgical castration is a task for the veterinarian. It can well be done at any time between the periods of her heat, but it must be remembered that it involves major surgery and that it is final. A spayed queen will be immune to the hysteria of her "calling," but never again will she produce progeny.

The Siamese tom or male cat is hardly less trouble than the queen. A healthy tomcat is in heat three hundred and sixty-five days a year and, while not so exigent to escape in search of a mate as is a queen in heat, may cause much trouble with his "spraying." The vile and malodorous musk from a tomcat is intolerable in the human habitation, and such a male kept for breeding purposes is best housed in some shed, cattery, or annex to the place of human residence. The Siamese male is less given to spraying of his musk than are other varieties of the domestic cat, but even he is not to be trusted indoors.

The pungent and unpleasant odor of his musk on furniture or draperies is well-nigh impossible to eradicate. The best means of controlling the stench is to wash with soap and hot water the material upon which the tomcat has sprayed after which it is best treated with a chlorophyl preparation. This process will alleviate the odor but will not kill it entirely, which only time can accomplish.

The male Siamese is the safest of all tomcats to keep in the house, but even with the Siamese, accidents (if spraying is deemed an accident) may occur. If kept in quarters adjacent to the house and those quarters are scrubbed and cleaned as may be required, the odor from the Siamese male is likely to cause little human discomfort.

But the Siamese male cat should not be permitted at large because of his fighting proclivities. He is the worst fighter in cat-dom. He will whip other cats twice his size, and is likely to be a terror to strange dogs. Towards dogs he knows and likes, he is prone to be at least amicable and even affectionate, eating from the same dish with them, sleeping in the same bed, and sharing their games and companionship.

Mighty fighter as the Siamese male may be, he does not always emerge from his fracases unscathed. He may be scarred, injured, or even killed, but he can not be subdued. He may come home of a morning *hors de combat,* but the following night is willing to return to the fray. His agility and quickness gives him an advantage over an antagonist much larger than himself, and he can be depended upon to give a good account of himself.

With all his proclivity to fight with other male cats, the Siamese tom is no less fond of human companionship than is the queen. There is none of the aloofness found in other whole tomcats in their human relations, and none of the scratching and biting of humans trying to handle or control a Siamese tom. A tomcat will follow his master from room to room, meowing and chattering all the while —a Siamese tom, that is.

And the Siamese tom does not molest young kittens as do the males of other breeds of cats. As a matter of fact, he appears to be truly fond of kittens and is interested and amused by them. While this is true as a rule, it is unsafe to give him access to young kittens without supervision at first to test his reactions to them. There is strong likelihood, however, that he will not willfully do them any harm. A Siamese tom that is banished from the house because of his spraying should be provided with a half grown kitten of either sex as a companion in his outdoor quarters. The two will become great friends and no harm will come to either of them. If such a kitten is a male, it should be removed from the adult tom before it comes to sexual maturity lest they fight; and if the kitten is a queen, she should be removed before her first calling season lest she be bred.

The neuter cat, by which is meant the castrated or "doctored" male, is the most satisfactory all-round feline pet. In it we are able to avoid the spraying and fighting of the whole male cat and the annoying periods of calling of the female. The neuter is gentle, affable, and companionable, and is perfectly clean and safe to keep in the house. It should, of course, be recognized that a neuter cat can not be bred from nor can his fertility ever be restored to him. A thoroughly first-class male should for that reason never be neutered, since the entire cat fancy is deprived of his services as a stud. A neuter is seldom so active as a whole cat, and his diet must be watched lest he grow fat and lazy.

The surgery of castration should be entrusted only to a qualified veterinarian, who will do the orchidotomy and return the cat to his owner usually on the following day. Castration of the male cat can be done at any age, al-

64

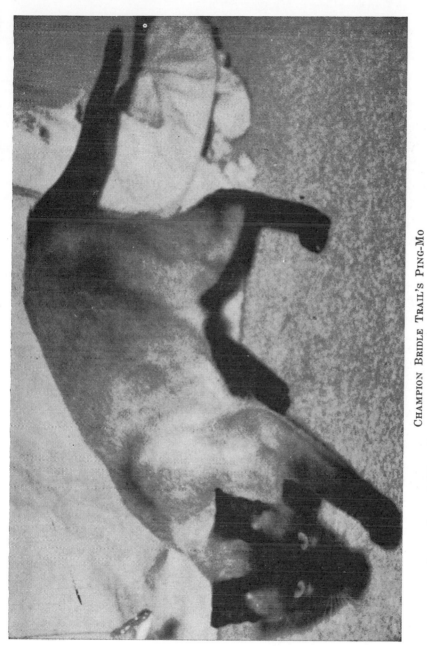

CHAMPION BRIDLE TRAIL'S PING-MO

A grandson of Silken Pedro, this outstanding specimen has sired 20 champions. He is owned by Mrs. John W. Hoag, Darien, Conn.

Left, Mo-Ling Sikkam.　*Right,* Ch. Ryecroft Sunya's Dream of Mo-Ling (Imp.)

Owner: Mrs. Max Fiedler, Co-Ling Cattery, Media, Pennsylvania.

CHAMPION ROSEBANK CHRYSANTHA ROYALIST
All-Southern 1950 Blue Point Siamese Female.
Owner: Mrs. C. Edward Voke, Norfolk, Virginia.

CABLE'S JEREMY, Seal Point Male

Sire: Dbl. Ch. Barnaby Cable II.   Dam: Fairchild's Ma Chere.
Breeder-Owner: Mr. and Mrs. R. A. Cable, Blawnox, Pennsylvania.

though it is unwise to have it done while he is in the process of changing from his milk teeth to his adult teeth. It should, of course, be done under local anesthetic. In England it is required by law that general anesthesia be used for the operation on cats more than six months of age.

The calling of the queen may also be stopped by having her spayed or castrated. This operation in the female requires major surgery and is more hazardous than the castration of the male, but usually safe and successful. To stop a queen from calling, a complete removal of all ovarian tissue is required, and not merely the severance or tying off of the fallopian tubes. Needless to warn, a spayed queen is permanently sterile.

One other characteristic of the Siamese as a breed is the preponderance of the number of males in most litters of kittens. In all the species of the higher animals, including all the cats, slightly more males than females are conceived; but no such ratio of males to females exists in other mammals as in the Siamese cat. In the aggregate, that ratio is perhaps as high as two to one. Most breeders have noticed it. In an occasional litter, it is true, it will be found that there are more females than males, but it is seldom the case. No explanation for the phenomenon is available, and it merits a biological investigation. It goes further toward the differentiation of the Siamese from other varieties of cats than any other single attribute of the breed.

Breeding Siamese Cats

EW problems arise to bother the breeder of Siamese cats. The principles are much the same ones that confront the breeders of other purebred livestock, but there are a few bits of advice and caution that may well be set down here.

The first of these is that the vitality and the vigor of the breeding stock must be absolute, and the more generations of vigor behind the cats employed for breeding, the safer the vigor of their progeny may be expected to be. This applies to all livestock, but it is particularly applicable to Siamese cats. The earlier importations were alleged to be frail, difficult to rear, unsound, and short-lived. This may have been true; or, on the other hand, the allegation may have arisen because of failure on the part of the fanciers to feed and care for the earlier cats properly, or because the earlier importations may have been carelessly or ignorantly bred and cared for in their native land. In any event, we know that the present day Siamese cats are as strong and easy to rear as cats of any other variety. It behooves breeders to maintain the vigor and livability of the race by breeding only from strong and vigorous stock.

Incidentally, in acquiring a cat, and especially a kitten, it is wise to make sure that it comes from a strong and viable parentage. The whole variety is not to be indicted for frailty and weakness just because a few careless breeders have failed to use care in the selection of breeding stock for stamina.

In the choice of breeding stock, one should consider the type and conformation of the prospective parents on both sides as well as the color patterns. Type tends to reproduce as readily as color. It must not be assumed that because a cat carries the colors of a Siamese that it is a true and purebred Siamese. It is known that many cats with the Siamese color patterns have admixtures of extraneous blood and are not real Siamese at all. It is wise to scrutinize pedigrees carefully to make sure that the cats it is proposed to employ for breeding are at least pure of blood.

It is never wise to balance a fault of one mate with an opposite failing of the other mate. For instance, assuming a queen is too short on her legs. Such a one should never be mated to a tall, gangling tom with the expectation of obtaining progeny intermediate in height between the two parents. It is much more likely that some of the kittens will be too tall and others too short of leg. It is much better to choose a tom of the correct station, after which one may anticipate that at least some of the kittens may be of correct height. The same principle applies to the length or roundness of head and face, and to other attributes of the correct type.

Siamese cats tend to darken in their colors as they grow older. They are ordinarily at their best in the matter of color when they are between one and two years of age. It is not to be feared that an older cat that has grown too

68

dark with age will transmit his intensity of color to his kittens. If he was of the correct shade at between one and two years, it is to be anticipated that his kittens may be of similar color at a similar age. A male cat at five years may be expected to produce exactly the same kind of kittens that he produced at one or two years. The same may be said of the female, except that she may not supply the nutrition to her kittens (both before and after their birth) in her older years that she gave her kittens in her youth.

Nor is it dangerous to breed from a cat at the time he is out of coat, if his shortcomings of coat are not caused by disease. Many persons believe that a cat transmits to his progeny the kind of coat that he carries at the time he is bred. This is not true. A cat will produce exactly the same kind of kittens when he is normally shedding his coat as he will produce at a time he is in perfect bloom.

The Siamese coat pattern is genetically recessive to that of whole colored or tabby cats. Therefore, two parents, both of the Siamese pattern will invariably produce kittens of that pattern. However, one Siamese parent mated to a self colored or to a tabby cat cannot be expected to produce any kittens at all with the Siamese pattern. These statements must suffice, since we have not the space at our disposal to discuss Mendelian genetic principles and to explain the reasons that the Siamese pattern, if derived from both sides of the house, will always breed true and why a Siamese mated to a cat of some other breed may never be expected to produce a single kitten with the Siamese color pattern. It will pay the breeder of Siamese cats, as the breeders of other kinds of livestock, to make himself familiar with the Mendelian laws and the science of genetics, books about which may be obtained at any book store or any library. Nobody can become a scientific breeder of any kind of animals without that knowledge.

Just as the Siamese pattern in general is recessive to the whole color or tabby pattern, so is the Siamese blue-point color recessive to the seal-point color. Blue-points will breed true if both parents are blue-points. Seal-point parents produce blue-point progeny only if both parents come from blue-point parents, and even then blue-point kittens can not be counted upon.

Of course, Siamese kittens are born white and attain their colors gradually. This must be borne in mind, since many a litter of purebred Siamese has been drowned at birth in the belief that white kittens indicate an accidental mating and in the expectation of the Siamese color pattern at birth.

Siamese kittens are usually born blind and open their eyes from the fifth to seventh day afterwards. This is earlier than is the case with most breeds of cats, which usually require nine to eleven days to open their eyes. Siamese are said sometimes to be born with open eyes, but it is the experience of breeders who have produced such litters that the kittens are defective and should be destroyed. The phenomenon is attributed to an insufficiency of vitamins and calcium in the diet of the mother while she has been pregnant. This writer has never had a litter born with open eyes and does not vouch for the allegations that such kittens are defective and not worth rearing; nor can this writer declare the cause.

Many books about the Siamese cat warn their readers never, never, never to in-breed or even to line-breed their cats. By in-breeding is meant the breeding together of two closely related cats, such as father and daughter, mother and son, full brother and sister, or half-brother and half-sister; by line-breeding is meant the mating of cats of more remote relationships, such as grandfather to granddaughter, grandmother to grandson, uncle to niece, aunt to nephew, and cousins one to another. This warning is due to a mistaken fear and to an analogy with forbidden incest in the human species. In-breeding *per se* is a harmless practice, as is line-breeding; and many of the finest specimens in all breeds of domestic livestock have been produced by those kinds of matings.

In-breeding should not be resorted to merely for its own sake, however, or for the sake of convenience. The breeder should do it only deliberately and when he knows what he

70

is about. It has been rightly said that "in-breeding is a two-edged sword." Soundly used it produces the best of results more quickly and surely than does any other method; wrongly used it results in disaster and is justifiably condemned. The writers who have warned their readers that it is never to be used are doing the breed a disservice, however altruistic their intent may be.

In-breeding merely intensifies the virtues and the faults of the stock which is in-bred, and it often brings to the surface faults latent in the remoter parts of the pedigree. It is true that it should not be employed with any but wellnigh perfect stock, the mates much alike in correct type and coloration, and above all with fundamental soundness, vigor, and stamina. If one has such desirable stock, one is safe to in-breed it intensely, generation after generation. That is the best way quickly to establish and confirm the excellence of what one has.

However, if one's stock is defective in type or lacking in vigor, to in-breed it is the acme of unwisdom. Much better to seek an out-cross of remotely unrelated mates. Little hope is held out to the breeder that by outcrossing he is likely to make great improvements or rapid strides in the betterment of his stock; but with atypical or weak stock it is better to out-cross than to in-breed.

The Siamese cat tends to run to a preponderance of males in the respective litters, and there are perhaps twice as many male kittens littered in the breed as there are females. There is no scientific way in which to account for this phenomenon. This is not to say that no litters are ever born of which all the members are females or in which females do not occur in greater numbers than males, but such are comparatively rare. In most mammals there is a slight preponderance of males at birth, but males are of the weaker sex and the proportions of the sexes in most species even themselves up and they are approximately equal.

There is no known practical method to influence the sexes of Siamese kittens or the young of any other species. One writer upon Siamese cats declares that she has been successful in obtaining kittens of one sex or the other by mating

71

her queens late or early in their heats. This is an old, old theory, long ago scientifically discarded as untenable. The "successful" writer may have obtained the results she claims, but the results have been merely fortuitous and in no manner depend upon the time in the queen's heat at which she was mated.

The comparative acidity or alkalinity of the female's vaginal tract has been believed to influence the sex of her progeny. This theory has also been discarded. No method of sex influencing is available, and we are compelled merely to accept the sexes of our kittens as they are born. It is true that the science of genetics explains to us, in its "X" and "Y" chromosome theory, how the sexes are respectively determined, but genetics offers us no means of influencing sex. We had as well save our efforts and devote them to something that is practically possible.

In the production of sound and viable kittens, the feeding of the queen during her gestation and lactation is quite as important as the mating of cats for good results. If at any time flesh foods—beef, mutton, horse-meat, and fish—are indicated in her diet, it is now. Above all must she have an ample supply of vitamins (all of them) and calcium.

It is impossible to mistake the time that the Siamese queen is in heat, for she may be depended upon to make the fact known by her persistent and insistent "calling" and her efforts to escape. Of course, she must be kept closely confined during this "calling" period and must be given access only to the tom with which it is intended that she is to be bred. Her determination to get away is profound and her stratagems to that end are subtle and endless. The queen may come into her first heat at any time after she is six months of age—usually somewhat later. It is usually unwise, both for her own sake and the sake of her prospective kittens to permit her to mate before she is fully mature, which should be at a year or a little less.

The tom with which she is to be bred should be carefully selected well in advance of the mating and all arrangements made with his owner. Assuming that the male and female are of different ownerships, the tom may be brought to the

72

CHAMPION VANGTAL OF NOR-MONT, Seal Point Male
Best Foreign Short Hair, Best Siamese, Best Seal Point and Best Short
Hair Champion at St. Petersburg, Florida.
Owner: Mrs. Merald E. Hoag, Nor-Mont Cattery, Arlington, Virginia.

DOUBLE CHAMPION AMMON RA'S LITTLE FAWN DA
Winner of the title, 1952 All Mid-Western Seal Point Female.
Began her show career at eleven months and completed her double
championship within three months. She placed first every time shown.
Breeder-Owner: Lillian Magner, Ammon Ra Cattery, Fort Wayne,
Indiana.

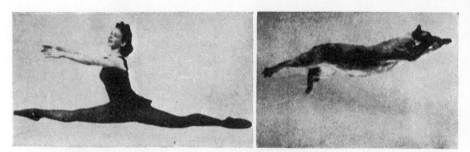

It *might* look like a split, but no foolin', here we have a *jete*. Off takes Jete, no slouch he.

Helen raises leg in arabesque. Aw—what's a one-leg arabesque? Jete shows how it's done with two back legs and a tail. And coming in for a landing, too. Much harder this way.

Once upon a time there was a cat (he is still there, never fear). He lived in a dance shoe store in a certain large city. Never had a dancing lesson in his life, or so his proud master, Jimmy Selva, says. But said cat was nimble, said cat was quick. And said cat, after years of delighting and convulsing dancers who came into the store with his feline terpsichories, heard about the marvelous Helen Wood, leading dancer in the musical, PAL JOEY, which opened in New York, vaunted to move with the speed, grace and trigger-fast responses attributed to the Cat.

"Anything she can do, I can do, too," meeowed Jéte. That's his name, and here he is, if you notice, challenging the marvelous Helen. At least, he tried.

Reprinted by permission Dance Magazine.

Helen in a *cabriole*. Ditto Jete. Note the turnout.

Helen in *demi-caractere releve sur la pointe* shields eyes against burst of light. Jete *relevees*, shielding eyes, nothing if not a *demi-caractere*.

To finish class, Helen unconventionally does handstand. Well! Jete rises to the challenge. In fact, he rises on one paw only. Class dismissed!

CHAMPION MILLBROOK PING PONG
All-Western Seal Point in 1951.
Owned by Mrs. W. Ball, Oakland, California.

CHUNG MUNG ABELARD and His Daughters, CHUNG MUNG NUI NUI and
CHUNG MUNG GRISETTE, Seal Point Siamese.

Owned by Philip Norman, Hollywood, California.
Program Director, Radio Station K N X.

queen or, much more usual, the queen taken or shipped to the cattery where he stands at stud. His owner should be advised of her arrival in advance of her coming that he may be prepared to receive her.

The mating itself is a simple process. The two mates should be introduced to each other through a wire partition to permit them to become acquainted before the consummation of their marriage. Before the ceremony, the claws of both should be blunted as much as is possible without touching the quick of the nails to forestall injury to either party. The room in which the breeding takes place should contain a bench or stool to which the tom may retire to escape from the tantrum of hysteria of the queen, which may occur after the breeding. One breeding service is usually sufficient; but a second may be given after the intermission of a few hours, better not later than one day after the first service. The queen must be closely confined after the breeding until she has gone completely out of heat, when the persistence of her calling will have ceased.

The care of the queen through her pregnancy is little different than at any other time, except that for the last four or five weeks she should be given more food but not enough to cause her to grow unduly fat and obese. The period of gestation is usually calculated at sixty-three days, but it is not absolute. It is usually shorter by a day or two in the case of young queens at their first pregnancy, but it may extend to sixty-eight or sixty-nine days without harm.

A week before the queen is expected to litter her kittens, a bed—a box with blankets—may be provided for her in some isolated and suitable place, and she should be introduced to it and, as well as may be, enticed to use it for the purpose it is intended. However, she may be expected to ignore the convenience provided for her and with a will of her own choose her place to have her kittens—a pile of clothes in the corner of a dark closet, an open dresser drawer, the floor behind the kitchen stove, or some other secluded spot which she deems fitting. Nothing is to be done about her choice except to permit her to have her way.

73

Littering kittens for a cat queen is seldom an ordeal. It will probably occur at night and the kittens will be found placidly nursing at their mother's breasts in the morning. The Siamese queen is so dependent upon human companionship that she may be grateful if her owner will sit beside her through the process of her parturition. The owner is well advised not to interfere in the birth of the kittens, however, unless he is an experienced expert. In the event that the queen is having undue difficulties in voiding her kittens, or if her labor is unduly prolonged, professional veterinary assistance is indicated. Amateur obstetrics is likely to do more harm than it does good. The queen may be depended upon to remove the kittens from the membranes in which they are born and to sever the umbilical cords. Nothing remains for the owner to do, except to change the bedding after the ordeal is finished. The less the kittens are handled or the mother is disturbed, the better off all concerned will be.

Equipment for the Siamese Cat

The Cat's Toilet Tray

IT IS recognized that cats are easily house-broken and are cleanly in the house, if given the opportunity to be so. This is especially true of the Siamese whose ready intelligence makes house-training easy. All that is required is a shallow box or large pan in which is kept some absorptive material into which the cat's excretions may be buried. This receptacle should be placed always in the same place in the house, and the cat should be shown it and at all times given access to it.

The absorptive material may be torn papers, sand, or fine peat moss. This should be renewed daily and the pan should be cleaned. The excretions of the cat are highly malodorous and the stench will soon permeate the premises unless the cat's toilet receptacle is kept scrupulously

75

clean. If the box or pan is moved from place to place, its new position should be shown to the cat, which, in the case of Siamese, at least, may be depended upon readily to accept the change and to accommodate itself to it. The Siamese is less a creature of fixed habits than most other cats.

There has recently come upon the market an absorbent material for the cat's toilet tray that is sure to be a boon to cat owners. This is marketed under various trade names, one of which is "Kitty Litter," and it is available at most modern pet shops. It has two advantages over the materials hitherto used for the purpose—first, it is impregnated with a drug which destroys odors, and, secondly, it may be disposed of by flushing it down the toilet. It is inexpensive and completely satisfactory.

Scratching Posts

Siamese are particularly active and are given at frequent intervals to what is called sharpening their nails. This clawing at the legs of chairs and tables, upholstered furniture and draperies, can be most destructive, and it is quite unnecessary. Long believed to be a natural process of conditioning the nails, it is now believed to be a method of tensing and stretching the muscles and tendons of the entire organism—a feline calisthenics.

Every cat should have a scratching post and be taught to use it and not to use other articles of furniture for the purpose. Such scratching posts may be purchased ready made for a nominal price at most pet shops, or one can easily be made at home. What is required is a two-by-four or a four-by-four piece of non-splinterable hard wood placed upright on a base that is not overturnable. Around the post is to be tacked a scrap of carpet solidly and securely. This carpet is to be lightly impregnated with oil of catnip which will attract the cat to it.

When the cat is discovered clawing at any other furniture

than its scratching post, it should immediately be taken to the scratching post, stood upright on its rear legs, and artificially induced to use the post. The cat must not be punished for its violations, but merely the post brought to its attention. A Siamese cat will soon learn what is expected of it and will use the post when the impulse to claw the furniture comes upon it. The catnip oil should be renewed from time to time upon the carpet of the post, although even if this is not done the Siamese may be expected to continue the use of the post once he has learned its purpose and that it is his own.

Toys and Playthings

A Siamese cat will get much joy out of its toys, and watching it play with them will afford much pleasure to the on-lookers. Of these toys one of the simplest and most enjoyed will be a small ball of woolen yarn, impregnated or not with catnip. It may be either loose or suspended by a strand to permit the cat to knock it about without displacing it.

Ping-pong balls and golf balls which the cat can knock about and chase are almost equally effective. Toy mice stuffed with catnip are favorite playthings. Tunnels which the cat can traverse, made of newspapers or paper boxes, afford the cat hours of amusement.

Whatever toys are used, if they are lightly coated with oil of catnip they will be more attractive and acceptable to the cat. Cats have an irresistible fondness for the odor of catnip, and some of them go into a veritable frenzy of joy when it is supplied to them after they have been long deprived of it.

Despite the fact that the cat is known to be color-blind, seeing objects as only black, white, and gray, one authority upon the Siamese declares that she has found her cats more attracted to red playthings than to those of any other color. How carefully controlled the experimentation has been the writer does not say. Without contradicting the statement,

77

the theory presents itself that it may be only the intensity and high saturation of the color rather than the color *per se* that intrigues the cat. This theory has been no more subjected to controlled testing than that of the writer who says that her cats prefer red. The alleged attraction to red is mentioned here only for what it is worth.

MINIATURE: CATS AND RATS
Page from the Lincoln Bestiary (MS. 81);
England, 1150-1200
Lent by The Pierpont Morgan Library

General Care of the Siamese Cat

OST CATS, it may be said, keep
themselves clean and the owner is not compelled to pay
any attention to their toilet. The cat is able to reach
well-nigh all parts of his external anatomy with his rough
tongue, and, since he is a very cleanly animal, he licks
and grooms his coat and skin every day so thoroughly
that dirt is seldom to be seen on him except as he may
be exposed to the smoke and grime of an industrial community. Some dirt he is just unable to get rid of by
himself and it becomes necessary for the owner to take
a hand in the cleaning process.

The Siamese is the shortest coated of the domestic cats
(except for the New Mexican hairless cat, which is now
believed to be extinct), and therefore the easiest of the
breeds to keep clean. It is to be admitted that its soft
undercoat is very dense, but it is so well protected by the

guard-hairs of the outer coat that it is not likely to become so grimy as the coat that covers it.

Usually the cat can be "dry-cleaned," by which is meant the thorough rubbing into his coat of some harmless dry powdered substance and just as thoroughly brushing it out again with the dirt, soil, and grease adhering to it. Substances suitable for such a purpose are fuller's earth, magnesia, chalk, talcum powder, Kaoline, and even flour or corn meal. This is most successfully done if the powder is permitted to remain in the hair for an hour or longer to absorb the oil with which all hair is lubricated. Such dry-cleaning may leave the coat apparently dry and lifeless for a day or two, but it is harmless and the hair will regain its lustre in a short time. The secret of the efficiency of the process is in the thoroughness with which it is carried out, both the impregnation of the hair with the powder and the completeness with which it is brushed out.

The alternative to dry-cleaning is the bath. Cats are notoriously not Baptists in that they are constitutionally averse to total immersion. This statement, however, does not of necessity apply to the Siamese as it does to cats of other breeds. In fact, many Siamese like to play in water and enjoy being bathed. Some of them hate and avoid water as do other cats. It depends upon the individual as much as it does with small boys and grown men.

A large dishpan or bucket is required, although a human bathtub will suffice, for the cat's bath. The water used should be pleasantly warm, certainly not hot, and should be as soft as it is convenient to obtain. The detergents which are marketed for the washing of clothes and dishes, such as Cheer, Tide, Joy (the latter a liquid), will be found better than soap, since they rinse away more thoroughly and easily. If soap is used at all, it should be mild and unmedicated, such as Ivory. The carbolated soaps that are sold as dog-soaps are dangerous for use on cats.

Set the cat gently into the water and after his coat is thoroughly saturated with water pour the detergent in a sufficient quantity down the length of his spine. Then with the ends of the fingers massage the detergent into

CHAMPION HOLLYWOOD BLUE VELVET

1950 A-W F ue Point Siamese Female who made history by being named
the Best at in the All Breed Show and Best Cat in the Siamese
Specialty Show at Denver in February, 1951. She repeated her
Specialty win this season, by again being named Best Cat
in the Denver Siamese Specialty in December.

Owned by E. W. Krampert of Casper, Wyoming.

Photograph by Frank Bjerring.

CHAMPION TELOT CABLE
Blue Point Siamese Female.
Owned by Mr. and Mrs. R. A. Cable, Blawnox, Pennsylvania.

CHAMPION NOR-MONT'S SIMI LEI, Blue Point and Her Babies
Breeder: Mrs. Merald E. Hoag, Arlington, Virginia.
Owner: Mr. and Mrs. Paul B. Gunnel, Jr., Silver Spring, Maryland.

SIAMESE KITTENS
The Blues are kittens from Nor-Mont Simi Lei, Seal Point is from
Nor-Mont Jade.
Owners: Mr. and Mrs. Paul B. Gunnell, Jr., Silver Spring, Maryland.

HYBRID PERSIAN-SIAMESE
Switzerland.

the coat until every hair is completely clean. After that, empty the soiled water from the receptacle and with a bath spray rinse the cat completely until all signs of the detergent are eliminated from the coat. Then dry the cat with a large bath towel, rubbing him freely and absorbing as much of the water from his coat as possible. In drying him, especial attention should be given to the ears, since moisture left in the ears may invite infection of those parts. Then place him on a clean towel or blanket in a warm room for an hour to finish his drying. Later he can be brushed.

If the cat objects to water, more drastic measures may be taken. They are not too kindly but, in necessity, are not inhumane. Place the cat in a bag of cotton cloth, head, tail, and all. A clean flour-sack is admirable for the purpose. This bag with the cat can then be soused through a heavy detergent solution, with several times the amount of detergent used in the ordinary bath. It can be massaged through the cloth without the hazard of the manipulator being scratched. The tub is then emptied and the cat, still in the bag, is thoroughly rinsed with the bath spray. This is a longer process than mere rinsing in the bath. The cat is then taken from the bag and dried as after the ordinary bath. The cat may not like this kind of bath, but if he is dirty he must submit to it.

Grain alcohol on a cloth or brush may be used for removing surface dirt from the outer coat, but it is not so satisfactory as an outright bath for cleaning a really dirty cat.

The Health of the Siamese

It is impossible for us to emphasize too strongly that the maintenance in perfect health and the freedom from disease of any domestic animal rests in final analysis upon its fundamental constitutional vigor. This is more true of the Siamese cat than of other cats or other animals. The Siamese cat when he was first imported into England from his native Siam had a reputation of being frail, difficult to keep in health, and short-lived. Despite the fact that the

Siamese is now a sturdy beast with his nine lives, his earlier reputation was perhaps well deserved. His ignorant Siamese breeders had neglected to select their breeding stocks for stamina and vigor, and had fed their cats for generations upon rice with a little fish. We can not wonder that the first cats to come into England and their descendants for several generations were sickly and unthrifty. Through rigorous discard of unsound breeding stock, the British breeders have reestablished the constitutions of the Siamese cat so that with a minimum risk we can now acquire a Siamese kitten with confidence that it will not only live but thrive.

However, we must still employ special care to select a kitten that is lively and well at the outset, one born from healthy and vigorous parents, sound and vital. With such a start in life, only normal and common sense care is required to keep the cat healthy and happy.

Of that care, the chief concern should be with the cat's food. The cat is first of all a carnivore. His food, almost his sole food, is meat. His dental formation is designed for the tearing of meat. His short intestine is not fitted for the digestion of large amounts of farinaceous foods or of roughage. However soundly he may have been bred, he must have meat if he is to thrive and to flourish. It is much better—and in fact cheaper—to provide the cat with a ration suited to his constitution than to force him to eat vegetable starches and require the frequent attentions of a veterinarian.

The meats suitable for a cat are beef, horse flesh, goat flesh, mutton, fish, all of them either raw or cooked. If cooked, the broth should be fed as well as the fibre of the meat. The small bones of fish should be removed, lest they puncture the stomach or intestines of the cat. The ration should contain about one-fifth of fat, for which purpose butter or margarine can be added to meat that is too lean, as horse flesh, for instance, is likely to be. The cat is especially fond of liver and kidneys, and they are especially good for him. A portion of liver may be added to his daily meals, or he should have one meal each week entirely of liver.

Milk is merely meat in another form. It is eminently suited as a ration for the cat, but it is not sufficient as an exclusive ration. One meal each day of milk is satisfactory, provided it is supplemented by another meal of solid meat or fish. Evaporated canned milk, weakened by an equal part of water, is quite as excellent as whole milk.

Some cats relish other foods, such as porridge and milk, mashed potatoes, or even green vegetables. A small portion of such foods may be given to a cat that likes them, but not until he has eaten his normal ration of meat. Most cats have no craving for these abnormal additions to their diets and prefer meat alone.

Every cat should have his vitamins artificially added to his food every day—all the vitamins, not just one or two of them. A tablet of multiple vitamins may be added to the milk or may be powdered and sprinkled upon the cat's food. In this manner the cat will swallow them and there will be no necessity to struggle with him and to force them down his throat. Vitamins are food; they are not medicine. All animals must have them. Before we were aware of their existence, we and all of our animals obtained the benefits of some vitamins in the food we ate, but we failed to obtain enough for the optimum of our nutrition. Our cats will thrive upon this small but important addition to their diets.

Another element in the cat's ration which is frequently neglected is the minerals, the only ones of which that require to be added artificially being calcium and phosphate, which may be in the form of a half teaspoonful of powdered di-calcium phosphate daily. This is tasteless. Ample iron and other mineral elements are obtained from red meats, and especially from liver.

It goes without saying that fresh, clean, and pure water should be available to the cat at all times. It should be changed at least daily. The cat may not appear to drink much of it, but it is essential that he have it any time he wishes to drink.

It would be idle here to go elaborately into the elements of food required by the cat—proteins, carbohydrates, and fats—since they are all required by all the higher animals. However, it may be said that the essential food of the cat is a balanced and complete protein food of animal origin. Given that and a modicum of fat with it, and the cat may be expected to be adequately nourished.

The breeding queen requires especial attention that she have all that she requires. Up to midway of her pregnancy, her usual adequate ration will suffice. After the fourth week of her nine weeks' pregnancy, her ration should be increased, both in quantity and in the supplement of vitamins and minerals. After her litter is born, it is difficult to give her too much food of which she requires more and more to supply the milk necessary to nourish her young. This food, however, should not be left before her at all times, but rather it should be offered to her at frequent intervals— as frequently as four times a day—and should be withdrawn from her after she has had the opportunity to eat her fill.

One may begin to feed kittens at three weeks of age, while they are still nursing their dam. By that time their minute teeth can be felt, which is an indication of their readiness to take food. This first food may well be of finely scraped beef which the kittens will take avidly. The first meal should be not more than a level teaspoonful, after which the ration may be rapidly increased until by four weeks they are receiving all they can eat. By that time it is no longer necessary to scrape the beef, since well ground hamburger will serve as well. The mother should be encouraged to suckle the kittens as long as she will; no food is better for them than their mother's milk. Kittens should be kept growing and some excess of fat on them is not at all harmful.

So far as concerns canned cat foods and other ready prepared cat foods that are on the market, it may be recommended that they be resorted to only in emergencies. It is wise to keep a small supply of them in reserve. However, most such prepared food contains an excess of carbohydrates

84

—especially the less expensive ones—and should be used only when meat is not available. Solid canned meats and fish are satisfactory as occasional meals for cats, but owners should be duly cautious about trying to maintain their cats upon the canned rations usually offered for sale as cat foods.

In general it may be said that a well fed cat is a healthy cat. No other element in the care of a cat contributes so much to his welfare as does an adequate diet. And an adequate diet is one largely made up of sound meat and fish. The soundly bred, fundamentally vigorous, and well fed cat has little fear of disease, which he can surmount, even in the rare cases in which he can not avoid it.

Fleas

The cat may become infested with any of several varieties of fleas, which, besides being extremely annoying to the cat, serve as intermediate hosts for the young stages of the tapeworm. It may, indeed, be said that the control of fleas on the cat is also the control of tapeworms, since cats are unlikely to be infested with tapeworms from any other source than fleas. The varieties of fleas that attack the cat are the human flea (*Pulex irritans*), the dog flea (*Ctenocephalides canis*), the sticktight or chicken flea (*Ctenocephalides gallinacea*), and, above all, the cat flea (*Ctenocephalides felis*).

There is little difficulty in freeing the cat from fleas; the real problem is in keeping him free from them. Fleas do not breed upon the cat, but rather in dust, dry sand, lint, and debris, from which upon their maturity they attach themselves to the cat. It is extremely unsafe to apply to the cat's coat or skin phenol or any of its derivatives or any insecticide which contains D. D. T. However, such controls may safely be used upon the premises in which the fleas breed, thus destroying the pests before they reach the cat. Even better is to sweep up and burn such accumulations as are possible breeding beds for fleas. Soil may be treated with kerosene with 10% D. D. T., or with sheep dip solutions containing phenol, or with lime-sulphur dip. This is preliminary to any treatment of the cat, which will prove futile unless the source of the fleas is brought under control.

The best and safest method to eliminate fleas from the cat's skin and coat is by the use of pyrethrum powder, an excellent form of which is marketed under the trade name of Buhac. This powder is entirely harmless and is safe to be used upon the youngest kittens. It is to be rubbed plentifully into the cat's coat and permitted to remain there from ten minutes to half an hour. Stunned fleas will fall from the coat and may be destroyed. It is to be remembered that pyrethrum does not kill the fleas, but only stuns them. In applying pyrethrum, it is best to keep the cat on a large paper or a bed sheet spread on the floor upon which the fleas may be caught and killed. Another method is to keep the cat in a dry bathtub during treatment, and from it the waste powder and fleas may be later flushed down the drain.

Pyrethrum may be less effective in the control of sticktight fleas than of other varieties. Sticktights are much smaller than other fleas and are likely to affix themselves tightly to the animal in black patches, frequently found on the ears, burying their heads in the cat's flesh. If forcibly detached from the animal, the heads of these fleas are often broken off to remain in the flesh to cause it to infect and fester. A plaget of cotton wetted with grain alcohol if applied to a patch of sticktight fleas will cause them to release their hold upon their host, whereupon they can be combed or brushed out and destroyed. Sticktight fleas are seldom found on cats that do not have access to neglected and dirty chicken houses.

Cats are less liable than dogs to infestations of lice and ticks, although they are not entirely immune to them.

Infections: Feline Enteritis (Cat Distemper)

Feline enteritis, although frequently but mistakenly called distemper, is distinctly different and to be distinguished from distemper as found in the dog. It is impossible for the cat to contract enteritis from a dog sick

86

with distemper or for a dog to contract distemper from a sick cat. The two diseases are, however, not entirely unlike, especially in that they are the major scourges respectively of the feline and the canine tribe.

Feline enteritis is an acute, infectious, highly contagious disease of cats, usually of young cats. It is also sometimes referred to as croupous enteritis, epizootic enteritis, malignant panleucopenia, infectious feline agranulocytosis, and feline typhus. It appears to be most prevalent during the cold damp weather of early spring and late autumn, although it may appear at any season, in any part of the world, and all cats of all breeds are subject to it. It is probable that the Siamese cats, when they were first brought to England and before they had been subjected to the rigorous selection for hardihood which they underwent at the hands of their British breeders, were among the most frequent victims of enteritis. However, the vigorous Siamese, bred from hardy parents, and well fed, is no more liable to contract this disease than a cat of any other breed.

Feline enteritis is considered to be the most serious disease encountered in cats and takes its greatest death toll among kittens and young cats. It often occurs as an epizootic (corresponding to an epidemic among human beings) affecting and rapidly decimating the entire young cat population in certain districts.

The disease is characterized principally by its sudden onset, highly contagious nature, rapid and violent course, profound alterations in the blood, its frequent fatal termination, and its predilection for young cats. Although the symptoms are variable, those most characteristic are high fever, loss of appetite, enteritis (acute inflammation of the intestinal tract), a marked decrease of white blood cells, rapid loss of flesh, great depression, diarrhea, vomiting, and sometimes a discharge from the eyes and nose. Affected cats manifest extreme soreness of the abdomen and may assume a characteristic position, lying flat on the belly with head lowered, forelegs spread laterally, and hindlegs stretched out. Roughening of the coat, complete

87

loss of appetite, sudden elevation of temperature, and depression are usually the first symptoms observed. These may be followed by severe diarrhea, the stool being sometimes streaked with blood, vomiting, extreme weakness, marked emaciation, complete exhaustion, and death.

The incubation period, that is, the time between exposure to the infection and the appearance of the first symptoms, is five to six days under experimental conditions and six to eight days or longer in natural infection. The course of the disease is usually very rapid, affected animals sometimes dying in twenty-four to forty-eight hours, and in especially acute cases, particularly in kittens, it is often so rapid that death may occur before any well-marked symptoms develop. Cases of this type, particularly when several cats in the same neighborhood are similarly affected, are frequently mistaken by their owners for poisoning. The mortality is high, often exceeding 80 percent.

Devitalizing influences that decrease the resistance of kittens, such as rickets, parasitic infestation (particularly hookworms), unsanitary, poorly ventilated quarters, and undernourishment, are predisposing factors to feline infectious enteritis. The causative agent is known to be a filterable virus. Natural infection may occur by direct contact of healthy with diseased cats or by exposure to contaminated quarters, bedding, utensils, or other articles that have been in contact with infected cats. There is considerable evidence that fleas may harbor the virus and there are definite indications that fleas may play an important role in the spread of the disease. The virus is said to be found in the urine, feces, and blood of infected cats and it is said to remain alive for a considerable length of time. It has been reported that virus maintained at room temperature has remained alive for as long as 91 days.

Various biological products (such as vaccines, antisera, and bacterins) are commercially available for use in the treatment and prevention of the disease, and reports from practicing veterinarians are that they have some value if promptly and properly used. Improvement in sick cats has been noted following the administration of repeated

88

large doses of homologous feline enteritis serum, and the administration of such serum appears to be the best prophylactic (preventive) measure for the protection of healthy cats during an epidemic of the disease. If treatment with serum is begun in the early stages of the malady before temperature begins to drop, it appears that a large percent of the infected cats can be saved. It is alleged that complete protection of young kittens against this disease can be obtained by the injection of prophylactic doses of two to three cubic centimeters of a serum obtained from immune adult cats that have been exposed to the disease.

No specific medicinal treatment is known for feline enteritis. Affected cats should be isolated and placed in comfortably warm, dry quarters. If animals show a disposition to take nourishment, a diet of broth, milk, and raw eggs should be supplied. The administration of biologics and drugs for the treatment and relief of affected cats should be undertaken only by a qualified veterinarian. Antibiotics, such as penicillin, terramycin, and aureomycin, may not arrest the feline enteritis itself, but may prove useful, at the discretion of a veterinarian, in forestalling secondary invasions of bacteria and other disease-producing organisms, which are all too likely to occur and to aggravate the disease.

When the presence of feline enteritis is suspected, the best thing to be recommended to the cat owner is promptly to consult a veterinarian skilled in the treatment of small animals and to accept and follow his advice rigorously. Feline enteritis is no disease for treatment by the amateur.

Hair Balls

Cats in licking themselves, especially at the time of their moulting, swallow considerable hair, which frequently compresses together into balls, causing intestinal impaction. The Siamese cat is little subject to hair balls, since his coat is so short that the hairs are not liable to compression into balls. The best preventive of hair balls is to keep cats well brushed at the time they are shedding their hair.

The treatment, if hair balls are suspected or known, is a dose of a mild laxative, such as paraffin oil or milk of magnesia together with a fast of a day or two. If the hair ball is not passed in the ensuing stool, an enema with soapy water may be indicated.

Rabies

Reference is here made to rabies not because the reader's cat is likely to be infected with it, but rather because the cat is not. The cat is, however, subject to that disease. Its rarity in the species is shown by the fact that there were only 207 cats recognized as rabid in the United States for the year 1938, and 209 for 1939, the last year for which such statistics are available.

Rabies is possible only when the subject is bitten by another rabid animal or when it has the saliva of a rabid animal injected into its blood-stream. This is highly unlikely with a cat that is not permitted to run at large, and rarely occurs even to the most errant of cats. Infected cats are prone to retire into a corner and resent intrusion upon their privacy. They may, however, show viciousness when molested.

There is no remedy for rabies, and the only thing to do with a cat known to be infected with the disease is mercifully to kill it or to isolate it and wait for it to die, which it will do in a few days after the first manifestation of the symptoms of the disease. Care must be taken not to permit an infected animal to bite children or other animals.

The literature about rabies, to which all warm-blooded animals are subject, is extensive; but, except to warn the reader of the remote possibility of its occurrence in the cat, there is no room here for the further discussion of this rare but horrible and surely fatal disease.

Fits, Convulsions, or Nervous Spasms

Common fits or convulsions may occur in cats of all ages, but are most common in young animals at the time of changing their teeth. A fit is not a disease in itself but merely a symptom of some other disorder, usually of an irritating nature. Violent exercise, nervous excitement, teething, indigestion, foreign bodies in the stomach or intestines, parasitic infestation (worms in the intestines or mange mites in the ears) are some of the common causes of fits. They may also occur during the onset of some febrile disease and sometimes appear to be of an hereditary nature (epileptic fits).

Attacks usually occur suddenly; muscular movements become uncontrollable and there is a rigidity affecting all the muscles and a champing of the jaws, with the appearance of frothy saliva about the mouth. The animal may finally fall on its side, kick violently, and lose consciousness. After a few minutes, it rises to its feet with a staggering gait and appears to be in a state of bewilderment. When symptoms of a coming seizure are noticed, or during convulsions, the cat should be moved to a quiet, dark room and left alone until it recovers. As a protection against bites and scratches during an attack, a cat should be handled only with heavy gloves or wrapped in a blanket.

After recovery, food should be withheld for a day, and a mild laxative, such as paraffin oil or milk of magnesia, should be given to clear out intestinal irritants. To prevent further attacks, attempts should be made to determine the cause of the trouble and to rectify it.

Metritis

Metritis is an acute or chronic inflammation of the uterus (womb) of the female cat, caused by the retention of the fetal membranes, infection introduced at the time of parturition, wounds of the mucous membranes of the vagina and uterus, or injuries. Cold and damp quarters are also conducive to the disease. In cats affected with acute metritis there are swelling and congestion of the vulva and vagina with a brownish or blood-stained fetid discharge from the vagina. Other symptoms are fever, loss of appetite, vomiting, and tenderness in the region of the uterus.

91

Treatment in mild cases consists in irrigation of the uterus with mild antiseptics. In severe cases, surgical treatment is often necessary to effect a cure. Such treatment is best entrusted to a qualified veterinarian.

Chronic metritis (*pyometra*), characterized by the collection of pus in the uterus, like the acute form, appears only after parturition. It is due to the same causes as the acute form. The principal symptom is the continuous discharge of grayish-red fetid pus from the vulva. Other symptoms are enlargement of the abdomen, emaciation, weakness, and a rough coat. Treatment is surgical and usually necessities the removal of the uterus and ovaries.

In both forms, injections of penicillin can be used to advantage, although it may not be expected to effect a cure without removal of the cause.

Eclampsia

Eclampsia is a nervous affection occurring in the nursing female and characterized by convulsions. The cause is not definitely known, but the condition has become established as due in some measure to a calcium deficiency. It may occur in the pregnant queen just before she litters, but it is more likely to manifest itself shortly after parturition.

The female animal that has ample calcium in her diet throughout her pregnancy is seldom subject to attacks of eclampsia. The surest cure is such prevention.

The attacks appear suddenly. The symptoms are first panting, excitement, and restlessness, followed by convulsive spasms; the animal falls on its side and may kick violently. The muscles become tense, breathing is rapid, the pulse is accelerated, mucous membranes are congested, and there is an increased flow of saliva. The cat remains conscious during an attack. The duration and severity of the spasm may vary, but affected animals should receive immediate treatment.

Intravenous injections of calcium gluconate is the most satisfactory treatment and should be administered by a veterinarian. Sedatives, such as morphine or nembutal, are of value in controlling the acute attack. The affected queen should be placed in warm, quiet quarters and should not be permitted to nurse her kittens during the attack or until completely recovered from it.

The female draws upon her store of calcium to supply the skeletal development of her young, both before and after their birth; and as a result, at a certain point in that depletion, the mother goes into spasms. Ample calcium in her diet forestalls such depletion, and intravenous calcium gluconate is the quickest way to restore the calcium drained from her system for the nourishment of her young.

Conjunctivitis and Other Eye Diseases

An inflammation of the membranes lining the eyelids is known as conjunctivitis or in the vernacular "sore eyes." It may be caused by irritants, injuries, or infections, or it may be one of the symptoms of some systemic febrile disease. It may first be noticed as a congestion and watering of the eyes, followed by the formation and discharge of mucous and finally of pus. The best remedy, which is usually successful, is to squeeze into the open eye a small amount of ophthalmic ointment containing penicillin, obtainable at any pharmacy. This treatment should be continued twice, better thrice, a day until the inflammation has abated. Alternative medications are ophthalmic yellow oxide of mercury (2%), freshly prepared argyrol (10% solution), or zinc sulfate (1% solution). Two or more of these remedies may be alternated in the treatment of severe cases. Borated petrolatum applied to the edges of the eyelids will prevent their being stuck together by the accumulated discharge.

Keratitis is an inflammation of the cornea—the normally transparent covering of the front of the eyeball—caused by wounds, the presence of foreign bodies and other irritants, the neglect of conjunctivitis, or the spread of inflammation from other structures of the eye. It may be mild or serious. The symptoms are lachrymation, extreme sensitiveness to light, and cloudiness of the cornea, indicated by the appearance of a bluish-white film. The measures employed in the treatment of conjunctivitis (above) will usually suffice, if they are taken in the early stages of the affection. Severe cases require the attention of the veterinarian.

Suppurative keratitis (ulceration of the cornea) usually occurs as an aggravation of simple keratitis, due to neglect of the condition at its inception. The ulcers when healed are prone to leave permanent scars and occasionally lead to perforation of the cornea and permanent opacity. Treatment is the same as for conjunctivitis although the attention of a veterinarian is indicated.

Cataract is a disease in which opacity occurs in the lens of the eye and its capsule. It may result from injury or some febrile disease, but it is usually produced by senility. It usually produces loss of vision. Surgery is the only remedy and it is seldom successful.

Ear Mange and Other Diseases of the Ear

Ear mange in the cat is caused by a small mite (*Otodectes cynotis*) which lives in the external auditory canal. The mites may be seen with the unaided eye, minute, slow moving, white objects, either in the ear itself or in materials removed from it. The mites are similar to those which produce sarcoptic mange on other parts of the body, but are larger and have longer legs. They are found deep in the canal of the ear, near the eardrum, where they puncture the delicate skin and feed on the tissue juices. Considerable irritation results from their presence, and the normal production of the ear secretions is interfered with.

The cat with ear mange scratches its ears, shakes its head and rubs the ears with its paws. Often it holds its head on one side, and may turn in circles or run in circles to show its unease. The ear canal becomes filled with inflammatory products and modified ear wax, interspersed with few or many mites.

Ear mange may be confused with inflammation of the ear

due to other causes, and it is necessary that the diagnosis be confirmed by microscopic examination of material removed from the ear canal before treatment is instituted.

The treatment consists of the removal or destruction of the ear mites. There are many means available to accomplish that purpose. Perhaps the simplest and one of the best is as follows: With cotton dipped in grain alcohol on the end of a match stick or orange wood stick, gently remove all exudates and debris from the cat's ears. Extreme care should be used not to injure the ears or to puncture the eardrums. When the ears are deemed to be as clean as it is possible to get them, an ointment made of ten parts of petrolatum to one part (by measure) of derris powder containing 5% rotenone, well mixed together, is injected into the ear canal, which is massaged externally to make sure that all the surface of the canal is thoroughly covered. Two or three such treatments, a week apart, should suffice to eliminate the ear mites and to clear up the ear mange.

The only other maladies likely to affect the ears of a cat are such as are due to injuries or bites from other cats. Open lesions should be cleansed and anointed with some antiseptic ointment such as Iodex, after which they are permitted to heal.

Diseases of the Skin

SARCOPTIC MANGE

Cats are less subject than dogs to sarcoptic mange, which is caused by the mite *Sarcoptes scabiei*, but cats are not immune. It is the most widespread disease of the skin caused by an external parasite. It is analogous, even if not identical, with scabies (the seven year itch) in mankind, and it is possible for humans to become infected from mange-ridden cats. Therefore, unnecessary handling of affected animals, especially by children, should be avoided.

Any morbid condition of the skin or coat may be popularly but mistakenly referred to as mange. However, mange and eczema or some other affection of the skin should not be confused, since mange is a definite and specific condi-

95

tion caused only by the invasion of the particular mange mite. To treat as mange some other condition is quite futile and is likely to result in harm. A microscopic examination of the scrapings from a lesion is the only certain way to diagnose mange.

The mange mite is so minute as not to be visible to the unaided eye. The male mite is harmless, but the adult female burrows under the skin and lays her eggs there. She and her young set up an irritation which results in much itching and discomfort to the cat that harbors them. The disease usually makes its appearance on the head— on the bridge of the nose—around the eyes, or at the base of the ears. Sometimes, however, it is first noted on the front of the chest, on the lower abdomen, under the front legs, or on the inner surface of the thighs, and if not treated the entire body becomes involved.

The first signs of the disease are red points which soon develop into small blisters. As the female mites burrow into the skin, there is an exudation, or discharge, or serum, which dries and forms a scab. The affected parts of the skin soon become covered with branlike scales and later with grayish crusts. Itching is intense. As a result of the animal's scratching and of the irritation caused by the mites, the skin becomes thickened and wrinkled. The frequent rubbing and scratching favor secondary bacterial infections and the formation of sores. The hair may become matted and fall out, leaving bare spots. Decomposition of the exuded serum gives rise to a peculiar mousy odor, which becomes more pronounced as the disease progresses. If the affection is allowed to go unchecked, the cat's digestion and other bodily functions become impaired, and death follows in a few months.

Sulphur ointment was the long accepted treatment for sarcoptic mange, but in many cases it has failed to bring relief. Derris ointment, such as is recommended for ear mange, is perhaps as satisfactory a medication as any other in the early stages of this disease. This is made by thoroughly mixing ten parts of petrolatum with one part (by measure) of derris powder with a 5% rotenone content. It

CABLE'S NI-SAN, Seal Point Female
Sire: Dbl. Ch. Knight's Nickleby. Dam: Ch. Par-Ami Cho Cho San.
Breeder-Owner: Mr. and Mrs. R. A. Cable, Blawnox, Pennsylvania.

GRAND CHAMPION NEWTON'S JAY TEE
The first and only Seal Pointed Grand Champion.
Owner: Mrs. Arthur C. Cobb, Newton, Massachusetts.

HYBRID PERSIAN SIAMESE KITTEN
From Switzerland.

This represents the result of a genetic experiment.
The first Long Haired Siamese to be developed.
The mother is Bobbit of Newton, a black Hybrid with her daughter,
Debutante of Newton. Out of eleven kittens, there were 3
long haired Siamese, 6 long haired Blacks and 2
short haired Blacks.
Breeder-Owner: Mrs. Arthur C. Cobb, Newton, Massachusetts.

should be applied freely to all lesions so as to embrace the surrounding areas. Treatment should be repeated every fifth day and a careful search should be made for fresh lesions on parts of the cat that have not been treated.

Another excellent treatment for isolated spots, one that stops the itching instantly and permanently, is the following: 2 parts grain alcohol, 1 part green soap, 1 part the best grade of Balsam of Peru. Mix the ingredients thoroughly in a bottle with a wide mouth and use the large cork as an applicator. The worst feature of this preparation is that it stains, but only temporarily.

For a severe case of mange that has been permitted to spread over large areas of the cat's skin, the following treatment has proved effective: Mix thoroughly 4 ounces of derris powder (containing 5% rotenone), 1 ounce of neutral soap, and 1 gallon of warm (not hot) water. Saturate the coat of the cat thoroughly and rub the solution into the hide with a stiff brush. Do not rinse the cat after treatment, but absorb the surplus wash with a towel and permit the remainder to dry in the coat or on the skin. Three or four such baths, spaced five days apart, should destroy all mange mites.

It is essential in the control of mange that all quarters occupied by the cat, all beds, all utensils, brushes, combs, toys shall be sterilized. It serves ill to cure the mange on the cat only to permit it to become reinfested with mites from articles with which it has been in contact before its treatment.

It may appear strange, but it is true that the surest way to prevent sarcoptic mange is by means of an adequate diet of meat, vitamins, and minerals. It seems apparent that the mange mite seldom gets a foothold upon a completely well nourished animal. It is not easily to be explained how adequate nutrition and ordinary cleanliness set up a barrier to the intrusion of an external parasite, but the fact remains that sarcoptic mange is very rarely found on cats that are given ordinarily good care.

Domedectic (follicular) mange is not believed to affect cats.

97

RINGWORM

Ringworm is a communicable disease of the skin occurring in cats and readily transmissible to the dog, man, or to other animals. The disease is caused by specific fungi (chiefly *Microsporon* and *Trichophyton* species), which are somewhat similar to certain ordinary molds. The lesions of ringworm usually appear on the face, head, or legs, but they may appear on any part of the body.

In cats the lesions are small, raised, scaly or scabby areas, usually almost circular, covered with hair, but detectable by running the finger tips over the skin. Microscopic examination and culture tests are necessary for an accurate diagnosis.

If treatment is started early, when only a few lesions are present, the disease can be cured in five or six weeks. Treatment consists in clipping the hair from around the lesions, removing the scabs and applying tincture of iodine or salicylic acid solution (5%) two or three times weekly until recovery takes place. Scabs and hair removed during treatment should be burned to destroy the infection. Due precautions should be observed in handling cats affected with ringworm because of the transmissibility of the disease to man. House cats and cats not permitted to run at large seldom have ringworm.

FAVUS

Favus is caused by a fungus known as *Achorion schonleinii*. It occurs principally in young cats and rarely in dogs. The sites most frequently affected are the paws, especially the skin of the toes near the claws, and the head and face. Lesions may, however, occur on other parts of the body.

The disease is characterized by circular yellowish or grayish patches that develop into thick layers of a crust of a sticky consistency.

Application of tincture of iodine or a 5% solution of salicylic acid are of value in the treatment. A relatively new drug, known under the names of griseofulvin or fulvivin, is reported to be useful in treating fungus.

Cats are so little subject to eczema—much less than dogs or humans—that it is not justifiable to treat that disease at great length in this volume. The important thing about eczema is that it is not mange and is not to be mistaken for mange. It is not infectious or contagious either to man or other animals, but it is stubborn and likely to be difficult to control.

Eczema occurs in two forms—in an acute moist condition, referred to as "weeping eczema," or as a dry chronic condition, which is more frequent. In the moist form the development of the disease is rapid. It is characterized by an intense erythema, marked itching, the formation of vesicles, a serous exudate, loss of hair, and a glistening, moist appearance of the skin. The chronic form is more leisurely in its development. It is characterized by inflammation and eruption of the skin, intense itching, loss of hair, and formation of scruff, crusts and scabs.

The most common site for the development of eczema is the region around the base of the tail and extending along the back of the shoulders and neck. The skin about the genital organs may also be affected. A moist form of eczema with a brownish discharge often affects the ear canals and the skin between the toes.

The disease is frequently complicated by secondary invasions of bacteria or other organisms into the lesions, and these may best be treated with antiseptic washes, ointments, and powders. The primary cause of the lesions does not respond to such treatment.

Indeed, eczema is not so much a disease of itself as it is a symptom that something is amiss in the cat's environment or regimen. What may be wrong is not in all cases easy to discover. It may be an allergy to certain foods or to certain things in its environment; it may be some dust or other irritant; intestinal parasites may produce it; it may be the result of too much or too little food; it is most likely to be a deficient element in the food, such as not enough of one of the vitamins or minerals, too much starch, too much or not enough fat. Only experimentation in altering the environment and changing the diet may determine the cause of the malady, and, once the cause is discovered and removed, the eczema may be expected to disappear as rapidly as it came.

Lip-Ulceration of the Cat

Ulceration of the skin of the upper lip is a condition peculiar to cats. It usually becomes chronic and does not respond readily to treatment. Good results are sometimes obtained by treating with iodine preparations, such as Iodex ointment. Application of silver nitrate (5%) has also been reported of some value.

In treating skin affections in cats, under no circumstances should soaps or disinfectants containing phenol, creosote, tar, creolin, or naphthol be used, as cats are extremely sensitive to these materials.

Intestinal Parasites of Cats

The varieties of the worms and other internal parasites that may affect the health of the cat are so numerous that we are able to find a place in this volume for the discussion of only the more frequently found ones. The ones omitted are so rarely found in the domestic cat that their inclusion would confuse the reader more than it would contribute to the well-being of any but the most unusual cat.

Tapeworms

The tapeworms that infect cats in the United States may be roughly divided into two general groups—the armed forms and the unarmed forms. Species of both groups resemble each other in having a head, a neck, and a chain of segments. In the armed forms the head is provided with four suckers and a rostellum, or prominence, bearing two or more rows of hooks. In the unarmed forms the head is provided with a pair of sucking grooves instead of suckers. There is also some difference in the genital organs

100

of the two forms. Both forms must have an intermediate host for their development in their larval stages, the armed forms requiring but one such intermediate host, and the unarmed forms requiring two. That is indeed the greatest practical difference as it pertains to their elimination and control in the cat.

Of the armed tapeworms, the only ones with which we are here concerned as frequently infesting cats are the double pored ones, technically known as *Dipylidium caninum*, which is the one also most often found in dogs and for which the intermediate host is the flea and the louse, and *Taenia taeniaeformis*, for which the intermediate host is the rat, the mouse, and other rodents. The one can be avoided in the cat by keeping the animal free from fleas and lice, and the other can be avoided by preventing the cat from eating rats and mice.

Of the unarmed forms of tapeworm the two most prevalent in the United States are *Diphyllobothrium latum*, the so-called broad or fish tapeworm of the Great Lakes region, and *D. mansonoides*, found in cats of New York and Louisiana. A third is of frequent occurrence in the West Indies, where it infests almost all cats in parts of Puerto Rico, but has not become established in the Continental United States. The first intermediate hosts of these three unarmed forms of the tapeworm are small crustaceans or crawfish-like animals, which to us is immaterial. But the second intermediate hosts in the case of the fish tapeworm are fish, and in the case of *D. mansonoides* the second hosts are amphibians, reptiles and some mammals. The cat that is not permitted to eat any of the second intermediate hosts raw can never have tapeworms of the unarmed forms.

The harm, if any, which the presence of tapeworms in his intestines does to the cat is disputed. It is known that some cats live happy and apparently healthy long lives while infested by tapeworms, and the suspected presence of tapeworm in the cat is no cause for immediate alarm. Of course, the humane owner does not knowingly permit his pet cat to harbor tapeworms indefinitely. Cats infested with tapeworm, especially with cat tapeworm *Taenia taeniaformis*, may show loss of appetite, transient diarrhea followed by constipation, excessive salivation, and, occasionally, persistent vomiting. In kittens, the abdomen may be distended, and the animal may exhibit evidence of acute abdominal pain. Such symptoms, however, may not manifest themselves.

Little is known of the effect on cats of infections with unarmed tapeworm. Usually no symptoms of importance are noted, but symptoms similar to those caused by the armed forms have been reported. Animals heavily infested for long periods of time with unarmed tapeworm are said to be definitely stunted and even after worming fail to regain weight.

For armed tapeworm the most satisfactory medication is perhaps arecoline hydrobromide. This drug, the active principle of the areca nut which in its powdered form has been so long employed as an anthelmintic, is a drastic purgative and acts within a few minutes to half an hour or so after administration. The treatment should be given in the morning after food and water have been withheld from the animal over night and the cat should not be permitted to eat for some three hours after treatment. It may be necessary to repeat the treatment in a week or two, since some of the heads may not be removed in the first treatment and regeneration of the tapeworms may occur.

For removal of unarmed tapeworms, oleoresin of male fern appears to be more satisfactory than arecoline. The drug should be given after a fast of eighteen hours and should be followed by a purgative after half an hour.

Both arecoline and male fern are toxic, and professional veterinary advice regarding the correct dosage should be sought before treatment is attempted. Cats are especially sensitive to the toxic effects of drugs.

Roundworms and Hookworms

The nematodes or roundworms, which include the hookworms as well as the larger roundworms, are the most injurious of all the parasites of cats and especially of kittens and young cats. They infest kittens at an early age (being sometimes present at birth) before any resistance to infection is acquired and may be responsible for the loss of entire litters.

Of the large intestinal roundworms affecting cats, there are two kinds, *Toxocari cati* and *Toxascaris leonina*, much alike in their appearance, life history and habits, and much like the large roundworm of man, *Ascaris lumbricoides*. They vary in length from 1½ to 8½ inches, the males being considerably shorter than the females. On being voided by the host animal, the worms tend to coil in a spring-like spiral, and apparently this is responsible for the name, "spool worms," frequently applied to them.

Large numbers of eggs are deposited by the female worms in the intestinal tract of the host animal, and these eggs are discharged in the feces. Under favorable conditions these eggs develop embryos in from two to six days. The larvae undergo the first molt in the egg and the egg is then infective. The infective eggs are swallowed by the host animal and hatching takes place in the first part of the small intestine. The larvae of *T. cati* penetrate into the intestinal walls, enter the blood stream, by which they are carried to the liver and thence to the lungs, and finally are coughed up and swallowed. The larvae of *T. leonina* penetrate deeply into the intestinal mucous membranes, where they undergo considerable growth. After ten days they emerge and escape into the intestinal cavity where they grow to fertile maturity.

These large roundworms are particularly injurious to kittens, which, since well-nigh all kittens harbor more or fewer of them, should be wormed at weaning age. The commonest symptoms of roundworm infection are unthriftiness, digestive disturbances, and bloating. The coat is dead and lusterless, and the breath may have a peculiar sweetish odor. Large numbers of roundworms may cause obstruction of the intestines and may even penetrate the intestinal wall. In heavy infestations the worms may wander into the bile ducts, stomach, and even the lungs and upper respiratory passages. The occurrence of large numbers of the larvae of *T. cati* in the lungs may cause pneumonia, especially in young kittens.

The best medicinal agent for the control of roundworms appears to be normal butyl chloride. This substance has largely superceded its chemically kindred substances, tetrachlorethylene and carbon tetrachloride, as a vermifuge since it has been found that normal butyl chloride is equally efficient in ridding the host of its roundworms and that it produces fewer unpleasant side effects.

Normal butyl chloride is administered in the following dosages:

½ cubic centimeter (8 drops) to cats under 3 pounds;
1 cubic centimeter (15 drops) to cats 3 to 5 pounds;
2 cubic centimeters (30 drops) to cats 6 to 10 pounds;
3 cubic centimeters (45 drops) to cats 11 to 20 pounds.

Hookworms are the most destructive of all the parasites of cats. Three species, *Ancylostoma caninum, A. braziliense,* and *Uncinaria stenocephala,* may be encountered, of which the first named is the widest spread and most likely to attack a domestic cat.

The hookworms are relatively small worms; the males rarely exceed half an inch in length, while the females are somewhat longer. The head end is curved upward and is provided with teeth or some other armature. The only certain way to distinguish between the different species is by microscopic examination of the head end, but that makes little difference to the practical cat keeper who is concerned only with their general recognition as hookworms and the methods of control.

The life histories of the hookworms are relatively simple. The females produce numerous eggs which pass out in the feces. In about thirty-six hours under favorable conditions a wormlike, active embryo has formed in the egg. In the course of three to six days the egg hatches and liberates the first-stage larva. In about three more days this larva molts, or sheds its skin, and becomes what is known as the second-stage larva, which again molts in about eight days to become the third-stage, or infectious, larva. Infection of the cat as the host animal takes place through the mouth or through the skin. When the larvae enter the host animal through the skin, they get into the circulation and ultimately reach the lungs, are coughed up, swallowed, and finally reach the intestines, where they develop to maturity. When the larvae are swallowed with contaminated food or water they pass directly to the intestine. After reaching the intestine the larvae undergo two more molts and become mature, eggs appearing in the host's feces in three to six weeks.

The symptoms of hookworm infection are largely due to the irritations of the small intestine caused by the bites of the worms, to the removal of blood, and to the bleeding that follows the bites. The anemia of hookworm infection is the result of loss of blood rather than of any toxin secreted by the hookworms. In the early stages of infection there may be digestive disturbances and diarrhea in which the feces are streaked with blood. In severe infections the diarrhea may be severe, and the feces may consist almost entirely of blood. A marked anemia, evidenced by the pale appearance of the mucous membranes of the mouth and eyelids, also occurs. Infected kittens and very young cats rapidly lose weight, their eyes are sunken, and there may be clearly marked symptoms of depression, resulting in death.

The hookworm most commonly found in cats is of the same species as the common dog hookworm, *Ancylostoma caninum*. However, it has been found that, despite its like appearance and its specific name, it is of a strain especially adapted to live in cats and not readily transmissible to dogs. Because cats are usually house pets and have cleaner habits than dogs, opportunities for acquiring heavy infestations are much less frequently observed in cats.

The treatment for the control of hookworm is exactly like that for roundworms: *viz.*, normal butyl chloride in the dosages set forth above.

Rickets

Rickets is a disease due to the failure of calcification of the bones. The clinical indications of rickets include lethargy and listlessness, arched neck, crouched stance, knobby and deformed joints, bowed legs, and flabby muscles. The changes characteristic of defective calcification in the kitten or young cat are most marked in the zones of growth of the long bones of the legs—at the junction of the end (epiphysis) and shaft—and at the cartilaginous junction of the ribs.

At such points there is a cessation of calcification with an excessive production of cartilage and a deposition of fat. In the more advanced stages there is evident lameness, and the entire bone becomes soft and is easily deformed or broken. The development of the teeth is also retarded.

The largest part of the crooked fronts, cow hocks, and bandy legs so often seen in adult cats is caused by the rickets they have had in early life as kittens or young cats. Rickets is easily arrested, but the damage it has done can not be rectified; it is possible only to prevent the skeletal condition from growing worse and to alleviate the pain which rickets causes.

Rickets is the result of improper nutrition—the absence of enough calcium and phosphorus in the diet together with a deficiency of vitamin D, which enables the organism to metabolize the calcium and phosphorus. This may be rectified by the addition to the diet of the lacking minerals in the form of calcium phosphate, about half a teaspoonful each day, and the administration of vitamin D in some form. An excellent source of vitamin D is one of the fish-liver oils, such as a high potency cod-liver oil of any of the better known brands. The dosage of cod-liver oil is impossible to state without knowledge of the potency of the particular brand to be used, but it need be no more than one teaspoonful a day at most. Most cats relish the fishy taste of cod-liver oil, which may be simply added to their food. (Fish-liver oils must be kept in cool places and protected from light to preserve their potency.)

Most adult cats, except pregnant and nursing queens, do not need additional vitamin D over and above what they obtain from a normal diet. It is, however, just as needful to supply additional minerals and ample vitamin D to queens during their pregnancy and their nursing periods as to growing kittens and young cats. Otherwise, not only will the skeletons of their unborn and born kittens suffer and perhaps develop rickets but the systems of the queens will be depleted of calcium and phosphorus in their efforts to supply the needs of their young. If the mother is properly supplied throughout her pregnancy and nursing with enough calcium, phosphorus, and vitamin D for her own nutrition and that of her young, those substances do not require to be added to the diets of the kittens until they are weaned, after which they should have these supplements in their rations daily.

It is barely possible that vitamin D can be supplied in harmful amounts, although there are ten thousand kittens that suffer from the need for vitamin D for every kitten that receives too much of it.

Cats Are Hardy Animals

It is not here intended to discourage the reader by the discussion of the ills to which cats are heir. The list of such ills could be prolonged to infinity, and only the most frequently encountered are mentioned in this book. However, the vigorously bred and adequately fed cat is a hardy animal, and one may keep cats for years and, except for roundworms in kittens, may never encounter disease in them. The Siamese cat was once considered to be a delicate animal but need no longer be accorded any more careful treatment than other cats.

In order to thrive, cats must be fundamentally robust and bred from vigorous parents. All cats require and deserve clean, dry, well ventilated quarters and ample food, and of the best kind suitable for feline metabolism.

107

It should be needless to say that cats should not be permitted to run at large, to fight, to associate with other stray cats, to contract infections, and to be struck down by automobiles. Little else is required for success with them.

With respect to the various maladies which cats may have, the best advice that can be given is in the case of serious illness or the suspicion of serious illness of a cat to consult a veterinarian promptly. Veterinarians are busy men and are not to be annoyed by calls for attention to frivolous and imagined ills of cats, but serious symptoms require immediate attention.